HOFMANNSTHAL

THREE ESSAYS

HOFMANNSTHAL

THREE ESSAYS

by

Michael Hamburger

BOLLINGEN SERIES

PRINCETON UNIVERSITY PRESS

The first two essays in this book are taken from Volumes Two and Three of Selected Writings of Hugo von Hofmannsthal, Bollingen Series XXXIII, *published in 1961 and 1963, respectively. The third essay originally appeared in* Hofmannsthal: Studies in Commemoration, *ed. F. Norman (Institute of Germanic Studies, University of London, 1963). All are revised.*

PRINTED IN THE UNITED STATES OF AMERICA
BY PRINCETON UNIVERSITY PRESS, PRINCETON, N.J.

CONTENTS

POEMS AND VERSE
PLAYS

POEMS AND VERSE PLAYS

I

Hugo von Hofmannsthal published his first poem in June 1890, when he was a schoolboy of just over sixteen, his first playlet or "lyrical drama" in the following year. Though not unprecedented, this early emergence of a poet was extraordinary enough; and it was made more extraordinary by the emergence at the same time of the critic and man of letters—under the pseudonyms of Loris, Loris Melikow, Theophil Morren, or, in one case only, Archibald O'Hagan, B.A. From the autumn of 1890 onwards, this schoolboy poet and man of letters was also to be seen at the literary meeting-places of Vienna, such as the Café Griensteidl, at first in his father's company, later with older friends or alone. To say that he mixed on equal terms with established writers is an understatement; for he was accepted at once not merely as a youthful prodigy and a writer of the greatest promise, but as a master of his art. "Here at last," Hermann Bahr wrote of this first impact in a book published in 1894, "here at last was someone who contained the whole age, for all its thousand-fold contradictions and conflicts, within his mind."

This first, predominantly lyrical, phase of Hofmannsthal's working life lasted for roughly ten years, the last decade of the century. Though he continued to write poems after this period, he himself considered his lyrical vein exhausted and thought only five of his later poems worth preserving in book form. Much has been made of this apparent break in Hofmannsthal's development and of the crisis to which it was due. The majority of those who admired the lyrical poet neither understood nor forgave the change; they felt about it much as Rimbaud's admirers might have felt if he had lived to become a member of the Académie Française. Hofmannsthal's fame declined; it was said about him that if he had died at twenty-five he would have been a great poet. This epigram, as wrong and foolish as it was cruel, is quoted only because it sums up a superficial view of Hofmannsthal which not only prevailed during the greater part of his later life but persisted long after his death, in 1929, and has only recently been corrected by the publication in Germany of a fifteen-volume edition of his works, supplemented by several volumes of correspondence. The insight and researches of Hofmannsthal scholars like K. J. Naef, Richard Alewyn, and Martin Stern have also contributed to a reappraisal that is still in progress; and a collection of Hofmannsthal's posthumous works, soon to be published for the first time, should shed further light on one of the most complex and enigmatic minds of the half-century.

If one thing has already become clear, it is that the whole of Hofmannsthal's work, from the first poems, playlets, and stories to the last librettos, essays, and plays, is linked by strong, though bewilderingly subtle, threads. Hofmannsthal himself traced such threads in notes on his own work, but there are many others which he was unable or unwilling to indicate. Every perceptive student of his works has been aware of them. To treat the poems and lyrical plays in isolation would be to perpetuate the legend of Loris, of the "young prince," the "marvellous boy" of the *fin de siècle*, of whom it was also said that he dipped his hand into a bowl of precious stones while he wrote his "jewelled" verse. (The real Loris went to school, sailed, played tennis, and toured Italy on his bicycle; his parents were far from rich.) It will be necessary to stress not only the uniqueness of the early poems and plays—and Hofmanns-thal's abandonment of his first media has a significance not confined to his personal development—but their relation to the whole of his work. Had this legendary Loris really ex-isted, his writings would still maintain their prominent place in German literature beside the contemporary work of Stefan George and Rilke: but for historical reasons, rather than for their enduring power to move and to disturb us.

The truth is that the early admirers of Loris saw only those facets of his poetry and prose which answered the require-ments of the age; above all, they saw him as the belated repre-sentative in Austrian and German literature of that aesthetic movement whose progress they had followed in France and England. Hofmannsthal's early essays on the Pre-Raphaelites, Swinburne, Pater, Wilde, on Vielé-Griffin and Bourget, his translations from Maeterlinck and D'Annunzio, and his as-sociation with Stefan George's *Blätter für die Kunst* did point to a genuine affinity with an international movement op-posed in various ways to mere Naturalism. What Hofmanns-thal's contemporary readers and interpreters failed to see was that, however preoccupied with the reigning antinomy be-tween art and life, even Loris, the real Loris, was as much in-tent on resolving the antinomy as the propagandists of a "con-sistent" Naturalism; but in a very different way. Even the critical essays of Loris bridge the gulf between aestheticism and Naturalism. Ibsen's plays are treated not as social documents, but as self-confessions; Barrès, on the other hand, is censured for lacking a "centre, style, form." Swinburne is praised for his "dionysian" fervour, but with this important reservation: "These artists, as I said, do not come out of life: what they produce does not enter into life." Throughout these early critical pieces Hofmannsthal shows only a half-hearted sym-pathy with the cult of decadence as such, much as he appreciates some of its artistic achievements. His marked preference for the English aesthetic movement from Ruskin to Pater was due to its habit of combining moral passion and social consciousness with the pursuit of beauty. Where these were lacking, Hofmannsthal disapproved, though he was still unsure of the grounds of his disapproval. A passing addiction to Nietzsche's vitalism is evident in several of the essays and reviews, then again a concern with the forms of social life, style in life rather than in art, pointing to Hofmannsthal's later solution of the antinomy between art and life, introspection and activity, individualism and community, in comedies at once realistic and metaphysical, explorations of the symbolism and mythology of manners.

If the critic was still unsure of his grounds—and this critic, too, was predominantly lyrical, delighting in the leaps and somersaults of the spontaneous *causerie*—the imaginative writer was far less so. His very first verse play, *Gestern*, written when he was seventeen, was at once lyrical and didactic, an expression of the moods of the age and a critique of the self-centred hedonism that was one manifestation of contemporary aestheticism. In *Der Tor und der Tod*, written in 1893, this critique goes farther and deeper—incomparably farther and deeper, too, than any theoretical or polemical critique of aestheticism, because it is a criticism from the inside. The aesthetic man is revealed as the man who, ultimately, feels nothing at all; and by placing him *in extremis*, face to face with death, Hofmannsthal uncovers a much more radical and universal paradox. Only one of his early verse plays, the fragment *Der Tod des Tizian* of 1892, seems to lack the didactic sting of the other works, and only because it was left unfinished. But more of this later.

The paradox I am trying to indicate here is that it is the early lyrical plays of Hofmannsthal, the very works that were

hailed as pure poetry in the sense defined by the French Symbolists and by Stefan George, which tended towards didacticism; and not even towards that didacticism into which the
advocates of art for art's sake were apt to fall despite their
creed—Villiers de L'Isle-Adam and George frequently did so
—but towards one opposed to the creed itself. The richness
and virtuosity of diction in these early plays, quite close at
times to the freedom of Symbolist verse, make the contradiction not less, but more, acute. It is hardly suprising that Hofmannsthal could come to regard *Der Tor und der Tod* as the
first in a series of morality plays continued much later by his
Jedermann (1911) and *Das grosse Salzburger Welttheater*
(1922). The paradox has something to do both with the "im-
passe of aestheticism"—Hofmannsthal's own phrase in an
early letter—and with the predicament of verse drama in his
time. *Das kleine Welttheater* is the outstanding exception; for,
having come to recognize the lyrical nature of his playlets,
Hofmannsthal no longer aimed at dramatic effects in this
work; it is, as he called it, a puppet play, a sequence of very
loosely interrelated monologues with no obvious moral frame-
work and no dramatic interplay of characters. W. B. Yeats,
who was faced with similar problems throughout his active
life, was to resort to a related form in many of his later plays;
but his *Plays for Dancers*, with their fusion of mime, music,
mask, and the spoken word, offer a still more revealing parallel with Hofmannsthal's opera librettos and ballet scenarios of
later years. Here it is important not to be misled by preconcep-
tions about genres or by Hofmannsthal's greater readiness to
affect an outward compromise with the requirements of the
stage. In essence and conception, these works are as esoteric
as those of Yeats, and both are late products of the Symbolist
tradition. Hofmannsthal rightly emphasized the connection
between his early lyrical plays and his librettos for *Die Frau*

ohne Schatten (1913–14), *Ariadne auf Naxos* (1910 and 1916), and *Die ägyptische Helena* (1926).

To explain the transformation of the "pure" poet into the "mere" librettist of later years, the dramatist who did not disdain such "humble" tasks as the adaptation of plays by Sophocles, Calderón, Molière, Otway, and Jules Renard, the writing of scenarios for Diaghilev and even for a film about the life and work of Daniel Defoe, I must turn back to the beginning. Hofmannsthal's precocity was a real one. In reading his letters of the early period one is struck by his astonishing capacity for receiving and absorbing disparate experience, so that his attitudes never remain fixed for long, but are perpetually modified, corrected, and strengthened by self-criticism. His openness to external influences of every order—including the aura of persons, things, and places, of institutions, ways of life, ways of thinking and feeling—was such as to amount to a danger. To take only the most obvious of relationships, the personal, he was always in danger of being fascinated, overwhelmed, and abused by those whose strength lay in their monomania, the one kind of strength opposed to his own. This danger was inseparable from his strength; and the "magical" inspiration of his early work was nothing other than the presentiment or intuition of a multiplicity and underlying unity which his later work could only embody in a corresponding multiplicity of media, themes, and forms. The difference, as he said, lay between "pre-existence" and "existence," between potentiality and realization, between the homunculus in his bottle—endowed with prophetic and magical faculties as in Goethe's *Faust*—and the mature man's need to particularize, to separate, and to distinguish, a need inseparable from involvement in active life. Where Hofmannsthal's later works remain fragmentary or imperfectly realized, it is nearly always because the conception is too complex to be subordinated to

8

the demands of the particular medium chosen, to be absorbed into the surface. So in the cases of his first prose comedy, *Silvia im Stern,* abandoned because too crowded with diverse characters and their intricate interactions, of the novel *Andreas,* the most tantalizingly enthralling of his many unfinished works, and, to a lesser extent, of his last tragedy, *Der Turm.*

All the hostility and misunderstandings to which Hofmannsthal's later work and person were subject arose from the prejudice that a writer so protean, so receptive, and so many-sided must be lacking in individuality and integrity. Yet even in the early poems and playlets Hofmannsthal's individuality had been nourished by his uncommon capacity for identification with what was not himself, whether experienced directly in his environment or indirectly in paintings, in the theatre, or in books. Unlike Yeats or Stefan George, he assumed no mask or anti-self, but relied on the social conventions to protect his privacy. "Manners," he noted, "are walls, disguised with mirrors"; and "manners are based on a profound conception of the necessity of isolation, while upholding—deliberately upholding—the illusion of contact." In the same way, Hofmannsthal could at once project and conceal his individuality by borrowing the artistic conventions of past ages; his refusal to draw a categorical line between "art" and "life," past and present, not only absolved him from the false dichotomies of his time but gave him a scope and a freedom that far exceeded the resources of direct self-expression. Needless to say, it also exposed him to the charge that he was a mere imitator of obsolete conventions, a receiver and renovator of stolen goods. Only the most minute attention reveals how much of himself he put even into adaptations of other men's works. His so-called translation of Molière's little comedy *Les Fâcheux* is a good instance; it is nothing less than a preliminary sketch for Hofmannsthal's own comic master-piece, *Der Schwierige.*

The escape of Loris from his legend and even the crisis re-corded in the Chandos Letter were by no means the only turning points in Hofmannsthal's development. His corre-spondence shows a marked change of style after the summer of 1892, when he left school to study law for a time, then Ro-mance languages and literatures. If Loris ever existed, it was only till July 1892, when Hofmannsthal was eighteen years old. The affectation of *fin de siècle* languor—the French term occurs in several earlier letters, like other modish phrases—of sophistication, preciousness, and intellectual coquetry, hardly appears after this early period. The analogy with Rimbaud, in any case, is a far-fetched one. Hofmannsthal had never been a rebel or a bohemian; as the only child of parents who approved and fostered his interests, he had no cause to revolt. Though he was to find it necessary at times to remind his father that he was, after all, an artist—and an artist far more bizarre than even his father knew—neither at this time nor at any time of his life did Hofmannsthal wear his art on his sleeve. The more sober tone after this summer had several causes; one of them is too important to be omitted here.

In December 1891, Stefan George, who was staying in Vienna, was introduced to Hofmannsthal in a café. The meet-ing was followed by others, by a hectic exchange of notes, and by two poems written by Hofmannsthal, who was at once flattered and repelled by George's impetuous demands for friendship and loyalty. At one point George sent a bouquet of roses into Hofmannsthal's classroom at school! His other pres-ents included not only an inscribed copy of his early *Hymnen* but a transcription in his own hand of Mallarmé's *L'Après-midi d'un faune,* made in Paris with Mallarmé's permission. If this was Hofmannsthal's introduction to the French poet's

work, the gift proved more than a token of his initiation into
the Symbolist fraternity. But George's behaviour was not
priestlike; in one letter he addressed Hofmannsthal as "my
twin brother," and begged him to save him "from the road that
leads to total nothingness." Hofmannsthal's replies became
more and more stilted and evasive; another meeting in a café
was cut short by Hofmannsthal, apparently because George
had kicked and sworn at a dog. Hofmannsthal refused further
meetings and returned some of the books sent to him by
George, who accused Hofmannsthal of insulting him and even
mentioned a possible challenge to a duel. Hofmannsthal offered a formal apology, but, when George renewed his ap-
peals, could no longer cope with the situation and had to ask
his father to intervene. All this within a month. A second,
seemingly calmer, phase followed in May, when George returned to Vienna and persuaded Hofmannsthal to become a
contributor to his periodical, *Blätter für die Kunst*. The two
poets continued to correspond until 1906.

The shock of this early encounter with an artist diametri-
cally opposed to him in temper and aims can be detected not
only in Hofmannsthal's letters but in several of his later works,
including his adaptation of Otway's *Venice Preserv'd*
(1902–4), which he dedicated to George. Doubtless the shock
was increased by the undercurrent of passionate courtship in
George's first advances; but it was George's intellectual and
moral demands—totally different from anything Hofmannsthal had known in his early friendships with Austrian writers
like Arthur Schnitzler, Richard Beer-Hofmann, and Hermann
Bahr—that left a deep imprint on his mind and work. Somehow George had succeeded in putting Hofmannsthal in the
wrong; it was the younger man who appeared as the traitor,
like Jaffier in *Venice Preserv'd*, enfeebled by that "molluscoid
impressionability and lukewarm susceptibility" of which

George accused the Austrian artists of the time. "It was my firm belief," George complained in 1902, "that we—you and I—could have exercised a most beneficial dictatorship in our literature for many years." Hofmannsthal's failure to enter into this partnership—on condition, of course, of a complete acceptance of George's literary programme, which virtually excluded all contact with the *profanum vulgus* not dedicated to the aspirations of the Circle—was ascribed to Hofmannsthal's "rootlessness"; and, accustomed as he was to social relations governed not by imperious demands for allegiance, but by tact and at least the appearance of mutual tolerance, Hofmannsthal was not always capable of the firmness and bluntness needed to make his own position quite clear. The extent of George's power over him, never as great as George wished or Hofmannsthal sometimes seemed to concede, is most apparent in his choice for a time of the title *The Reflections, the Cut Stones, and the Speaking Masks* for the projected collection of his poems later published by George; this title, modelled on those of George's books, was reduced to the unpretentious *Selected Poems* before the collection appeared in 1903.

Another effect of the encounter with Stefan George, which assumed a kind of archetypal character for Hofmannsthal, as the first and extreme instance of several others that were to follow, was a gain in self-knowledge. Hofmannsthal began to understand his own need for an organic relationship with society, not for a dictatorship of the artist over his public, but a relationship essentially reciprocal. This need, he also recognized, was distinctly Austrian rather than German; and he became increasingly concerned with the distinction. "Was George stronger than I?" he reflected in a letter of 1919: "I don't know, there is too much that's artificial about him, *and he leaves out too much.* In any case, since my eighteenth year I have behaved quite consistently towards him, outwardly placing myself—not him—at a distance, for I had no use for the position of a *coadjutor sine jure succedendi* which he offered me pantomimically; all that was too German-fantastic for my taste—too bourgeois, ultimately and deep down."

Hofmannsthal's humanism—quite different again from George's ideal of an artistic élite, with its hierarchy of fastidiously but arbitrarily selected exemplars—assumed the peculiarly Austrian form of a desperate attempt to reconcile all the component parts of a disintegrating culture, to re-integrate them rather than subordinate them, and to find that centre which alone could resist the tendency of things to "fall apart." To that centre, difficult to define but easy to sense in his writings, Hofmannsthal was committed with a fervour and a constancy that survived all his defeats; but everything was against him. In a centrifugal age the most fantastic and monstrous progamme issued by any faction, sect, or party was more likely to attract adherents. The influence of George's exclusive circle radiated outwards, to the universities and the youth movements and into political life, though with consequences neither foreseen nor desired by its begetter. Hofmannsthal, one of the few writers of the time whose political views were determined less by personal prejudice than by a painstaking study of history, political theory, and current affairs, had to be content to be the representative of a "society that does not exist." At once liberal and mystical, because rooted in his early intuition of the unity within all diversity, his humanism lacked the appeal of those final solutions offered by the extremists of every colour. Yeats summed up the dilemma once and for all; but, though a gentleman according to Yeats's definition of the gentleman as "a man whose principal ideas are not connected with his personal needs and his personal success," Hofmannsthal did not "lack all conviction," only the "passionate intensity" of monomania.

This dilemma became more acute, and incomparably more painful, in Hofmannsthal's later years, especially during the first World War, when he undertook several missions of a semi-political kind, and in the post-war period; but his poetic crisis at the turn of the century had a social aspect touching on the dual function of language as self-expression and as a means of communication, and this linguistic crisis, too, was anticipated in many of Hofmannsthal's earlier works, both imaginative and critical. What he called his "word-scepticism" and "word-mysticism" are equally striking in an early book review, *Eine Monographie* (1895): "For people are tired of talk. They feel a deep disgust with words. For words have pushed themselves in front of things. Hearsay has swallowed the world. . . . This has awakened a deep love for all the arts that are executed in silence." So much for the "word-scepticism"; the "word-mysticism" is its corollary: "For usually it is not words that are in the power of men, but men who are in the power of words. . . . Whenever we open our mouths, ten thousand of the dead speak through us." Though a peculiar ambiguity characterized Hofmannsthal's attitude to the social function of language—and indeed to society in general—it is this social aspect of his linguistic crisis that lends it a more than personal significance. The difficult transition from the Romantic-Symbolist premises to a new classicism, or from individualism to a new impersonality, to put it differently, has confronted most of the major poet-dramatists of this century, from Claudel and Yeats to Eliot and Brecht; and the problem posed so succinctly and drastically in Hofmannsthal's Chandos Letter was an inescapable one.

It is a characteristic of Hofmannsthal's works of every period, even the social comedies, that the most crucial thoughts and feelings of his personages cannot be rendered in words, only intimated by gesture, music, or silence; the conventions of speech are masks that conceal more than they convey, or ciphers that must be translated into a medium other than words. "Form is mask, but without form neither giving nor taking from soul to soul," Hofmannsthal wrote; and he meant not only form in works of art but the conventions that govern speech, manners, and appearances in life, the phenomenalizing principle. In the early lyrical plays the problem is avoided more often than solved, because they represent characters who have not yet learnt to face it; Claudio, the closed man, is only the extreme instance of a total incapacity to give and take.

Poetry, of course, had once had the power to combine both functions of language; but while lyrical poetry "aspired to the condition of music," dramatic poetry—the public medium—had not evolved a satisfactory substitute for the rhetorical modes of past ages. After abandoning purely lyrical media, Hofmannsthal continued to experiment with adaptations of classical drama, both ancient and modern, before arriving at three distinct, or at least separable, solutions: the allegorical morality play, the fusion of words with music in opera, and the fusion of realistic dialogue with a concealed symbolism. Each of these solutions has its parallels in the practice of other poets—in Claudel's religious and Brecht's political drama, in Yeats's plays that draw on the Japanese Noh conventions, and in Eliot's comedies—and each is an attempt to arrive at a public medium as far removed from outmoded rhetoric as from the complacent trivialities of Naturalism.

"To introduce profundity into the mundane": thus an unpublished jotting defines the distinction at which Hofmannsthal aimed as a writer of comedies. His correspondence with Richard Strauss provides ample comment on the symbolism of

15

his librettos. Hofmannsthal, in fact, was a penetrating critic and interpreter of his own works; and it may be that a writer so complex could not hope to be understood without his own help, which was largely withheld in his lifetime because he loathed self-advertisement and put his faith only in what was "formed." Certainly his part in the operas—that of a poet willing to sacrifice his immediate inspirations, though never his basic conceptions, to the requirements of a highly specialized and recalcitrant craft—was constantly belittled, if not despised as a concession to the vulgar; and his practice of "concealing the depth in the surface," the mystical core of his plays in their social trappings, tended to perplex the mundane while antagonizing the professedly profound. Yet to bridge the gulf between private vision and social involvement, the language of ecstasy and the language of practical life, was no compromise on Hofmannsthal's part; it was his primal need, and the necessary fulfilment of his lyrical pre-existence, to be achieved at whatever cost to his happiness or his reputation. The Servant's speech in *Das kleine Welttheater* prefigures the later course:

> *Mit dem ungeheueren Gemenge,*
> *Das er selbst im Innern trägt, beginnt er*
> *Nach dem ungeheueren Gemenge*
> *Äussern Daseins gleichnishaft zu haschen.*

> (With the vast and multitudinous tumult
> That's within him, he begins to clutch at
> All the vast and multitudinous tumult
> Of the outward world, its correspondence.)

II

Hofmannsthal's rejected title for his book of poems has the merit of indicating something of their character; the excessively precious "cut stones" rather less so than "reflections"

and "speaking masks." The last division, which he preserved
in later editions under the heading "Figures," is the most telling of all; for, essentially lyrical though it is, his early work
aspires to the condition of music or painting on the one hand,
to the condition of drama on the other. Two influences on his
early poetry mark the two directions: the musical lyrics of Ver-
laine, the dramatic monologues of Browning. Little more than
its length distinguishes *Das kleine Welttheater* from the
"speaking masks" or *personae* included among the poems, and
indeed it is less dramatic than the brief *Idylle* of 1892. All the
early playlets contain passages that could be printed as separate poems, even where they are not recognizable variants of
short poems which Hofmannsthal wrote and published as
such.

The significance of masks for Hofmannsthal, as for Wilde,
Yeats, George, and other poets of the time, has already been
touched upon. The development of the persona form by Yeats,
Rilke, Ezra Pound, T. S. Eliot, and Gottfried Benn would
yield further interesting comparisons. What is immediately
clear is that the persona or dramatic monologue answered a
need common to most of the major poets of the late Symbolist
and post-Symbolist periods; and the one kind of poem not to be
found in Hofmannsthal's various selections from his early
work is the poem of direct self-confession. Hofmannsthal did,
in fact, write such poems in the early years—the revealing
Für mich of 1890 is a notable instance—but he never included them in any collection that appeared in his lifetime.
Here the "molluscoid" Austrian proved more severe than the
intransigent purist George, who did not exclude the literal
"I" in the same way, though he also resorted to personae in
many of his longer cycles. The difference is one not so much of
subjectivity and objectivity—all lyrical poetry must combine
both to succeed—as of the degree of empathy shown in the

poet's projections of himself. In his capacity for self-identification, not only with the "figures" of his poems and verse plays but with things, situations, and atmospheres, Hofmannsthal was much closer to Rilke than to Stefan George.

Of the poems that aspire to the condition of music, none is more memorable than *Vorfrühling* (*Before Spring;* 1892). A literal metaphrase—to use Dryden's valuable term for the most humble of his three kinds of verse translation—will serve to explain why such a poem cannot be rendered at once literally and poetically.

Es läuft der Frühlingswind *Durch kahle Alleen,* *Seltsame Dinge sind* *In seinem Wehn.*	The spring wind runs through bare avenues; strange things are in its blowing.
Er hat sich gewiegt, *Wo Weinen war,* *Und hat sich geschmiegt* *In zerrüttetes Haar.*	It has rocked itself where there was weeping, and nestled in ruffled hair.
Er schüttelte nieder *Akazienblüten* *Und kühlte die Glieder,* *Die atmend glühten.*	It shook down acacia blossoms and cooled the limbs which, breathing, glowed.
Lippen im Lachen *Hat er berührt,* *Die weichen und wachen* *Fluren durchspürt.*	Lips in their laughing it has touched, and scoured the soft and awakened meadows.
Er glitt durch die Flöte *Als schluchzender Schrei,* *An dämmernder Röte* *Flog er vorbei.*	It slipped through the flute as a sobbing cry, and flew past the red of twilight.

Er flog mit Schweigen	In silence it flew through whis-
Durch flüsternde Zimmer	pering rooms and, descend-
Und löschte im Neigen	ing, extinguished the lamp's
Der Ampel Schimmer.	faint gleam.
Es läuft der Frühlingswind	The spring wind runs through
Durch kahle Alleen,	bare avenues; strange things
Seltsame Dinge sind	are in its blowing.
In seinem Wehn.	
Durch die glatten	Through the smooth, bare av-
Kahlen Alleen	enues its blowing drives pale
Treibt sein Wehn	shadows;
Blasse Schatten.	
Und den Duft	And the fragrance which it has
Den er gebracht,	brought from where it has
Von wo er gekommen	travelled since last night.
Seit gestern Nacht.	

In German, *Wind* is masculine; the English translator is faced at once with the alternative of neutering the wind or introducing an artificial personification. Yet the wind's sex is inherent in the conception—even deities and spirits are male or female—as is the analogy with the *pneuma* of inspiration and hence with the poet's mind, which touches on this and that, links one thing to another, gathers everything but retains nothing more substantial than a fragrance. The theme of the poem, in so far as it has a semantic theme, as distinct from a musical one, is the intuition of the multiplicity and unity of phenomena and of their correspondences; but these correspondences are established not by argument, as in Baudelaire's famous sonnet on the subject, the fountainhead of Symbolist poetry, but by Hofmannsthal's choice of the wind as the unifying factor, by the wind's passage through diverse phenomena, and by their organization into a pattern of rhythms and sounds. Alliteration and assonance, rather than similes, intimate the connections; by the recurrent *ü* sounds, for instance, of stanzas two and four, short in *zerrüttetes* and *schüttelte* (the ruffling and the shaking), long in *-blüten, kühlte, glühten, berührt,* and *gespürt.* To a very considerable extent, this poem was written by the German language itself; and, but for alliteration and assonance, quite a number of the epithets would not have occurred to the poet. Such effects cannot be rendered in another language, any more than the poem's lightness, that quality of happy improvisation exemplified by the change in its rhythm and rhyme scheme in the last two stanzas.

Not all the poems, of course, can be so easily classified. The *Lebenslied,* for example, can be read as a pure lyric like *Vorfrühling* or as a "reflection" rendered in a curious concatenation of symbols. Attempts to analyze and interpret these symbols have not convinced me that the poem as a whole has any but the vaguest meaning in rational terms. According to Dr. Carl J. Burckhardt, a close friend of Hofmannsthal's in his later years, Hofmannsthal pointed out to him that the lines

> *Der Flüsse Dunkelwerden*
> *Begrenzt den Hirtentag*

> (The rivers' darkening shine
> Binds up the shepherd's day)

are not an "incomprehensible ornament, but a perfectly straightforward observation of nature, familiar to every huntsman and farmer"—namely, that the surface of water remains bright when the rest of a landscape has grown dark—but went on to speak of the analogy between this phenomenon and a man's last thought, which "gathers all the light of day." This particular image, therefore, would seem to be related semantically to the references to death in the first stanza; and, in the notes and aphorisms which he called *Ad me Ipsum,* Hofmannsthal also commented on the special significance of evening in his early works, citing the conclusion of *Ballade des äusseren Lebens* and his playlet *Die Frau im Fenster*. Another of these notes is a comment on the last lines,

> *Die schwebend unbeschwerten*
> *Abgründe und die Gärten*
> *Des Lebens tragen ihn.*

> (The buoyant gulfs of blue
> And this life's gardens too
> Support him to the end.)

of which Hofmannsthal writes: "The meaning of the world is detachment. In worldly things nothing can be made fast. The world is a workshop, the place where things are shaped, the place of memory, change; it exists for the sake of the fulness of beauty, for the sake of love, etc." But here—as elsewhere in *Ad me Ipsum*—Hofmannsthal is reading later convictions into his early work. His Neoplatonic interpretation of the lines does not take account of the sheer arrogance which one can feel to be part of the gesture of this poem—the exuberant arrogance of the poet as magician. Nor did Hofmannsthal offer a detailed and comprehensive explanation of the poem as a whole, and I am not suggesting for a moment that he was under any obligation to do so. Though the poem undoubtedly says something about a certain attitude to the past, present, and future, to life and death, it is permissible to doubt that the eagle, lamb, and peacock have a strictly emblematic or heraldic function, or that Hofmannsthal attached an intelligible meaning to each of these animals. This is not to argue that others should not discover or invent such a meaning; but whatever current critical dogma may prescribe on the point, there is no compelling reason why a critic should know more about a poem's meaning than the poet knew. The degree of irrationality in a poem is one of its intrinsic and authentic qualities; it should be recognized and respected, not explained away.

As an imaginative gesture and a musical composition, the poem needs no justification; as an elaborate cryptogram, it will continue to provide the most strenuous exercises in ingenuity.

This brings me up against a vexed question which it would have been pleasant to leave alone: I mean the question of Hofmannsthal's mysticism in these early years. That he experienced uncommon states of exaltation, of communion with inanimate objects—very much like those which Rilke recorded in verse and prose—even of trance-like estrangement from his circumstantial self and kinship with the absent and the dead, proves that he had the disposition of a mystic; and his concern with the duality of phenomenon and essence, time and timelessness, flux and constancy, is the concern of mystics. Yet he himself was honest enough to distinguish between the disposition and the vocation, the poet's "magical" faculties and the mystic's dedication not to the state but to the object of communion. It was this honesty that compelled him to abjure his magic when he had come to regard his illuminations as a mere concomitant of the "lyrical state" (the term is his own), as a psychic, not a mystical condition. In a very early prose fantasy, *Gerechtigkeit* (1893?), the poet's feeling of kinship with the whole of creation is judged by an angel and dismissed as specious. According to *Ad me Ipsum*, the Chandos Letter describes "the situation of a mystic without a mystique" —an excellent description of all the poetic creeds, such as Rilke's, which base a metaphysical system on the poetic process itself.

How strongly Hofmannsthal was drawn to such a creed, and how desperately he resisted the attraction, is shown not only in the Chandos Letter but in many earlier and later works. The so-called "Chandos crisis," as I have suggested, was not confined to a brief period; it goes back to the beginning of Hofmannsthal's work, and recurred frequently to the end. There is the splendid early story, *Das Märchen der 672. Nacht* (1894), intimately related to the poems and the playlets, of the rich merchant's son estranged from his life of contemplation, idleness, and luxury, drawn despite himself into the lives of his servants, into sordid and terrifying adventures, and to his death. "Like the horror and the deathly bitterness of a nightmare forgotten after waking, the weight of their lives, of which they themselves knew nothing, dragged down his limbs." It is not the servants' lives in themselves, but the young man's projections on them, that destroy him, because he has not found the bridge from his mode of existence to theirs. (Bridges, like fountains, wells, and rivers, are among the recurrent symbols in Hofmannsthal's early work.) And this allegory points forward to *Die Frau ohne Schatten* of later years. Everywhere the life of detached contemplation is contrasted and linked with the life of active involvement, the two modes of *Reiselied* and of *Manche freilich*.

> *Manche freilich müssen drunten sterben,*
> *Wo die schweren Ruder der Schiffe streifen,*
> *Andre wohnen bei den Steuer droben,*
> *Kennen Vogelflug und die Länder der Sterne.*
> . . .
> *Doch ein Schatten fällt von jenen Leben*
> *In die anderen Leben hinüber,*
> *Und die leichten sind an die schweren*
> *Wie an Luft und Erde gebunden:*

(Many truly down below must perish
Where the heavy oars of ships are passing;
Others by the helm up there have dwelling,
Know the flight of birds and starry countries.
. . .
Yet from their existence falls a shadow
Reaching the existence of those others,
And the easy are to the burdened
Bound, as to earth and air, together:)

Thus, in one of Hofmannsthal's early "speaking masks" or persona poems, *Der Jüngling und die Spinne* (1897), the two states are juxtaposed subjectively. The young man's ecstatic sense of being upborne by the cosmic powers is interrupted by his observation of a spider. What he felt to be communion with the whole of life now strikes him as a self-induced ὕβρις, the true nature of life being "to suffer pain, to inflict pain." As in many other crucial passages in Hofmannsthal's early work, it is an animal that works this change, so that even the conversion is brought about by an act of imaginative self-identification. If animals stand for the physical existence of men, their exposure to natural processes, the obtrusive reality of the spider has much the same function here as the "burdened" in the other poem. The arrogance of the lyrical state reaches its peak in the poem *Welt und ich;* and in *Der Jüngling in der Landschaft* it is contrasted with the religious life of service that was Hofmannsthal's alternative to it.

The purely subjective bridge over this dualism is empathy, that magical faculty which Hofmannsthal possessed to no less extraordinary a degree than Rilke. The Chandos Letter recapitulates the magical phase: "To sum up: In those days I, in a state of continuous intoxication, conceived the whole of existence as one great unit: the spiritual and physical worlds seemed to form no contrast, as little as did courtly and bestial conduct, art and barbarism, solitude and society; in everything I felt the presence of Nature, in the aberrations of insanity as much as in the utmost refinement of the Spanish ceremonial; in the boorishness of young peasants no less than in the most delicate of allegories; and in all expressions of Nature I felt myself." This empathy extended to animals and things: "A pitcher, a harrow abandoned in a field, a dog in the sun, a neglected cemetery, a cripple, a peasant's hut—all these can become the vessel of my revelation." Lord Chandos' feeling for the rats which he had ordered to be poisoned was "far more and far less than pity; an immense sympathy, a flowing over into these creatures, or a feeling that an aura of life and death, of dream and wakefulness, had flowed for a moment into them—but whence?" Yet the rats were poisoned all the same; and this is where Hofmannsthal's critique of poetic empathy links up with the linguistic crisis recorded in the same work. The cult of the merely aesthetic word—the word incapable of being translated into action and of "entering into life"—is rejected as altogether too easy. Only Hofmannsthal's later Platonism made it possible for him to come to terms with what he had come to regard as a pseudo-religion at best.

Hofmannsthal's own retrospective interpretation of his early work in *Ad me Ipsum* and elsewhere need not be taken as the last word on the subject; but since I am concerned with the whole of his development—in so far as it can be summed up at all in a brief study—even the more drastic of his later comments are relevant. The last persona to speak in *Das kleine Welttheater* is the Madman; and it seems that at the time of the Chandos Letter Hofmannsthal had already begun to consider the "lyrical state" in the light of psychopathology, and to relate it to the case histories recorded by the new psychological writers of various schools. His library contains the first edition of *Studien über Hysterie*, by Freud and Breuer (1895), works by the French psychologists Janet, Georges Dumas, Fulgence Raymond, and Gustave Le Bon, as well as many later works by Freud, Jung, Adler, and lesser-known writers on the subject. Two other books must be mentioned in this connection, because they were much marked and annotated by Hofmannsthal and served as sources for his own imaginative works: William James's *The Varieties of Religious Experience* (1902) and Morton Prince's *The Dissociation of a Personality* (1905). Hofmannsthal's most intense occupation with these and other psychological works falls into a later period, like that with the thought of Kierkegaard (though the three books by Kierkegaard extant in his library are German editions of 1886, 1890, and 1903 respectively); but, granted that the crisis did not begin and end in 1902, and considering that Hofmannsthal's friendship with Rudolf Kassner provided another contact with Kierkegaard's thought, both these influences must be taken into account. In *Ad me Ipsum* Hofmannsthal identifies the "word-magic" of his pre-existence with introversion and traces his gradual progress towards true existence in his own works. A comment on his poem *Weltgeheimnis* (1894) is almost startling in its psycho-analytical rigour. The poem begins:

> *Der tiefe Brunnen weiss es wohl,*
> *Einst waren alle tief und stumm,*
> *Und alle wussten drum.*
>
> *Wie Zauberworte, nachgelallt*
> *Und nicht begriffen in den Grund,*
> *So geht es jetzt von Mund zu Mund.*

(The deep well knows it still; once all were deep and dumb, and all knew about it.

Like magic formulae, babbled off parrot-wise and not fully grasped, now it passes from mouth to mouth.)

Hofmannsthal quotes the first line, and adds: "—in which the deep well is to be understood as the own self." Amongst other things, the "Chandos crisis" was one akin to that rendered by W. B. Yeats in *The Circus Animals' Desertion*—a very late poem, fortunately for him and for his readers. Hofmannsthal, as a Viennese, could not easily escape the pervasive influence of depth psychology, which caused him to reduce the cosmic mystery of his poem to "the foul rag-and-bone shop of the heart."

Needless to say, Hofmannsthal did not fall into the narrow rationalism which his comment may suggest, any more than Yeats did; he grappled with the new science of the subconscious with the same open-mindedness with which he faced the facts of economics or biology, not in order to embrace any simplifying orthodoxy—sex, money, or self-preservation as the *primum mobile*—but to correct and transcend his own inherited specialization, the deliberate irrationalism adopted in self-defence by a whole generation of poets at odds with the age. Hence the renunciation of a kind of poetry that was to become more and more deeply immured in its self-generated magic; a renunciation that can be judged as a loss of nerve or as a sacrifice, according to the point of view. What is important to note is that Hofmannsthal did not turn against this kind of art, or any other, but merely found its extreme developments unacceptable for himself. Whether we say that he feared for art or that he feared for society makes little difference; his fear, in any case, sprang from the awareness that the two are interdependent. With great patience and labour, Hofmannsthal proceeded to build his bridge from pre-existence—that "glorious but dangerous state," as he called it in *Ad me Ipsum*—to existence. The aesthetic man was not discarded in favour of the ethical or the religious man, as by Tolstoy in his anti-artistic fury at about the same time, but made to evolve, the whole man moving at once; and the true mysticism was sifted from the false. The subjective magic of the "lyrical state" now appeared to Hofmannsthal not only as a prefiguration of the complexities and conflicts of active life—a stage to be passed, not forgotten or rejected—but as the revelation of a different order of reality above and beyond the scope of active life; and indeed the themes of his early poems and plays, stripped of their purely personal implications, reached their climax in the political conflicts of one of his last works, *Der Turm*.

Nor did Hofmannsthal retract his views on the nature of poetry. His *Gespräch über Gedichte,* a dialogue discussion of Stefan George's *Das Jahr der Seele* published after the Chandos Letter, in 1904, and read with deep admiration by Kafka at the time, still insists on empathy as the source and substance of lyrical verse, though on an empathy that truly grasps its object, instead of using it as a mere stimulus for introspection. "If we wish to find ourselves, we must not descend into our own inwardness; it is outside that we are to be found, outside." This is one of the many points of contact between Hofmannsthal's conception of art and his ethical convictions; his mystical affirmation of love in the later works rests on the same insight. "None of us possesses his own self: it is wafted at us from without, escapes us for long periods and returns to us in a breath. And self indeed! The word is so little more than a metaphor!" Then follows a definition that anticipates Rilke's more famous one, in his comments on the *Duino Elegies,* of men as the "bees of the Invisible," gathering the honey of the visible world to store it in "the great golden bee-hive of the Invisible." What Hofmannsthal says is: "We are no more than dove-cotes"; and he does not deceive himself or his readers by pretending that the doves are engaged in some transcendental business. "And from all its transformations, all its adventures, from all the abysses and gardens"—an echo of the *Lebenslied*—"poetry will bring back nothing more than the quivering breath of human feelings. . . . How, from any abyss of the worlds, could it bring back anything more than human feelings, when poetry itself is nothing more than the language of men!"

Neither here nor elsewhere was it Hofmannsthal's purpose to belittle poetry or expose its pseudo-mysticism as a kind of imposture; what he wanted was to recognize and praise it for what it is. His essay holds fast to the basic premise of his own early work, "that we and the world are not different things." Because this is so, he also defends the essential freedom of Symbolism, the freedom of image and metaphor: "Never does poetry put one thing in place of another, for it is poetry, above all, that feverously endeavours to put the thing itself. . . . That is why symbol is the very element of poetry, and that is why it never puts one thing in place of another: it utters words for the sake of words; that is its magic. For the sake of the magic power that words have to stir us bodily and to transform us incessantly." In defending the aesthetic function of poetry for its own sake, Hofmannsthal also makes it the agent of a transformation that cannot be exclusively aesthetic, because the human mind is not divided into hermetically sealed compartments.

Hofmannsthal's difference with the absolutists of aestheticism was not over the belief in the autonomy of the work of art—a belief inseparable from the practice of Symbolism, and thus from his own practice at every period—but over the belief in the autonomy of the artist. Though rarely formulated, this was a common assumption; and to Hofmannsthal it was one of those aberrations of individualism in contemporary life and literature which he had opposed ever since his early essays and playlets. Even the new depth psychology served him as a means of overcoming self-absorption. Yet for a long time his own psychological relativism weakened his criticism of the *mal du siècle,* as soon as he tried to formulate it in theory. His word-mysticism ("the word is mightier than he who speaks it," he wrote in 1919) and his growing indifference, if not hostility, to the cult of individual talent as an end in itself, did not become firmly grounded in metaphysical beliefs. *Ad me Ipsum* has an epigraph from St. Gregory of Nyssa: "He, the lover of highest beauty, believed what he had already seen to be only the faint copy of what he had not yet seen, and desired to enjoy the original itself." But even in *Ad me Ipsum*, as we have seen, Neo-Platonism and modern psychology entered into a somewhat precarious alliance.

Both the early work and the late rest on Hofmannsthal's presupposition that "we and the world are not different things"; yet there is a third factor missing in this identification, and it is this factor that distinguishes the early work from much of the later. The connecting link between ourselves and the world—a link indispensable in the early works—is named in one of the *Terzinen*:

Und drei sind Eins: ein Mensch, ein Ding, ein Traum.

(And three are one: a man, a thing, a dream.)

In pre-existence, it is the dream that affects the identification of the man with the thing; and the dreamlike quality of the early work—nowhere more immediate or more powerful than in the story of the merchant's son to which I have referred—made the identification incomparably easier than it became in those later works in which Hofmannsthal confronted the intricate realities of social life without the aid of a magical or fairy-tale convention.

One of the "reflections" included among the poems purports to deal with the "outer life," but it does so from the point of view of a man roused from his dream. The extraordinary weariness and detachment of its enumerations— admirably conveyed by the recurrent "and," with which the poem also begins—corresponds to the imagination's judgment on reality. In the *Ballade des äusseren Lebens* the identification of the man with the thing has broken down, at least in the opening stanzas; their treatment of the phenomena of the outer world shows the reverse side of Lord Chandos' "continuous intoxication," its hangover. Where the mediation of dream is withdrawn, the things of this world are emptied of all meaning. This is the general dilemma of Symbolist poetry; one thinks of Mallarmé's description of the outside world as a "brutal mirage."

Yet in Hofmannsthal's poem the meaninglessness is redeemed. From Novalis' *Hymns to Night* to Rilke's nocturnes, evening has been the time when dream replaces perception, the heart takes over from the head, to mend all that daylight has severed. As a comment on the line

> *Und dennoch sagt der viel, der »Abend« sagt*
>
> (Yet he says much who utters "evening")

Hofmannsthal refers to a passage from J. J. Bachofen's book on "mother-right" in the ancient world: "Hesperus who brings together all that Eos has divided (Sappho, fr. 95; Catullus 62. 20 ff.), who brings the chicks back to their mother, brings quiet to all the hill-tops (Demetrius, *De elocutione* 141); he shines to Sappho as the gentlest and loveliest of all the silver stars in the vault of heaven." But this does not exhaust the significance of evening in the poem; evening is also

> *Ein Wort, daraus Tiefsinn und Trauer rinnt*
> *Wie schwerer Honig aus den hohlen Waben.*
>
> (A word from which grave thought and sadness flow
> Like rich dark honey from the hollow combs.)

The time of day is also an age of man. If in *Vorfrühling* and another poem, *Vor Tag*, the season and the hour symbolize pre-existence in the sense of potential existence, here it is to its other, more truly mystical, aspect, the intuition of past experience, that the time of day alludes. The German word *altklug*—which Hofmannsthal used in an early letter to describe his first playlet—conveys the sense of "precocious" as an anticipation of the wisdom of old age. Psychologically, the two aspects of pre-existence are related in the way in which the premonition of life is related to the recollection of life. As Wilhelm Dilthey demonstrated in Hofmannsthal's lifetime, imagination and memory are very closely connected. Memory was the Mother of the Muses; and, at its most truly mystical, pre-existence approximates to Plato's anamnesis.

> *Erinnrung ists*
> *Die Götter aus uns macht—*
> *Ich fühls, so jung ich bin . . .*
>
> (It's memory
> That turns us into gods—
> Young though I am, I sense it . . .)

—Cesarino says in Hofmannsthal's play *Der Abenteurer und die Sängerin* (1899), opposing this intuition of his youthful pre-existence to the adventurer's belief that "the moment is all." Recollection and premonition have the same power to act as "bees of the Invisible" and fill the hollow honeycombs of outer life. To say that it is only the anticipation of life, or only the recollection of life, that gives meaning to it, amounts to much the same thing; the meaning of life, in either case, resides not in its phenomena but in what lies behind them —or in what our imagination makes of them. The difference is a crucial one; but Hofmannsthal's early works are open to either construction.

Even if we decide that it is not a Platonic idea, but a purely subjective state, that fills the hollow honeycombs of outer life, anticipation and recollection are the processes that characterize Hofmannsthal's pre-existence. From the point of view of non-involvement in life he could extend the same sympathy to the very old as to the very young; so to the grandmother figures in two of his playlets, and the persona of *Des alten Mannes Sehnsucht nach dem Sommer.* The very old, like the young, the Lunatic, the Lover, and the Poet of *Das kleine Welttheater,* stand at one remove from that transitory life which Hofmannsthal had not yet learnt to accept or to penetrate except in imagination, memory, and dream. To these Hofmannsthal was to oppose the "non-mystical way," "the way to the social as the way to one's higher self," as he put it in *Ad me Ipsum;* and he specified three means of attaining this higher self, "through deeds, through one's works, through one's children." Yet the sacrifice demanded by this way also entailed a danger: "To act is to give oneself up." Hofmannsthal's adventurers succumb to this danger. "The decisive factor," therefore, "lies not in action, but in loyalty. The identity of loyalty and destiny." The higher life must "come about through the proper fulfilment of one's destiny, not through dream or trance."

It was this dependence on the mediation of dream that Hofmannsthal came to regard as the predicament of the late Romantic-Symbolist generation to which he belonged.

> New dreams, new dreams; there is no truth
> Saving in thine own heart . . .

—W. B. Yeats wrote in his early *Song of the Happy Shepherd;*

> Dream, dream, for this is also sooth.

The poems in Yeats's *Crossways* (1889) and *The Rose* (1893) are poems of pre-existence precisely in Hofmannsthal's sense of the word. Where Yeats resorts to dialogue or persona forms in these early books, the resemblance to Hofmannsthal's poems and lyrical plays is especially close, as in these lines from *Anashuya and Vijaya:*

> . . . And, ever pacing on the verge of things,
> The phantom, Beauty, in a mist of tears . . .

The dominant mood of Yeats' pre-existence is melancholy, as that of Hofmannsthal's is elation; but whether the phantom Beauty is captured through a mist of tears or through a haze of ecstasy, it can be captured nowhere but on "the verge of things." In Yeats's early work, too, the life of action and the life of imagination or contemplation are contrasted everywhere. Hofmannsthal's regal Gardener in *Das kleine Welttheater* has an exact counterpart in Fergus of Yeats's *Fergus and the Druid*:

DRUID: What would you, Fergus?

FERGUS: Be no more a king,
> But learn the dreaming wisdom that is yours. . . .
> A king is but a foolish labourer
> Who wastes his blood to be another's dream.

As in Hofmannsthal's *Ballade,* this dreaming wisdom opposes the flux whose symbol is the river or the road; and it matters little whether it is attributed to age or youth, since its essence is the same non-involvement in active life:

FERGUS: I see my life go drifting like a river
> From change to change; I have been many things . . .
> But now I have grown nothing, knowing all.

In images remarkably similar, both poets turn to

> . . . the loveliness
> That has long faded from the world;
> The jewelled crowns that kings have hurled
> In shadowy pools, when armies fled . . .

Both poets went on to resolve the dualism of life and art by means of an esoteric philosophy on the one hand, active involvement in life on the other, not without difficulties and ambiguities in either case. By resorting to an "anti-self" and other deliberate constructions, Yeats succeeded in making the transition from pre-existence to existence in lyrical poetry, as Hofmannsthal did not. Yet *Des alten Mannes Sehnsucht nach dem Sommer,* one of the few later poems which Hofmannsthal included in his own selections, shows how close he was to the step which he did not take. Its colloquial diction—a characteristic, too, of some of the earlier poems, such as the *Ballade,* but to a lesser degree—and its realistic imagery point in the same direction as his dramatic work of the same period. Lyrical drama, as its paradoxical name implies, was even more inextricably trapped in the predicament which I have tried to outline. Lyrical poetry could, and did, survive even where it did not yield an inch of its esoteric ground; lyrical drama could survive as poetry, but not as drama. The fate of Yeats's verse plays on the English stage is the sad proof.

III

"My main incentive is not to let bygone ages be wholly dead, and to make people feel what is remote and alien as closely related to themselves," Hofmannsthal wrote to a friend about the Chandos Letter, intimate confession though it undoubtedly was; and it was one of his habits to make such detours in time or space in order to arrive at himself. His many borrowings from other writers served the same purpose. From the very start, the dramatist in Hofmannsthal was distinguished from the lyrical poet not only by his moral and social preoccupations, but by an uncommon capacity for grasping and rendering historical "ambiances," chiefly through his highly developed visual and pictorial sense. In the earliest playlets (not given in this selection) the function of the historical setting is little more than the incidental one of providing picturesque effects. "At the time of the great painters" is our significantly vague clue to the Renaissance background of *Gestern* (1891); but the scene is described in exact and elaborate detail, and the Savonarola-like figure Marsilio—an embodiment of the bad conscience of aesthetic hedonism, like many similar figures in contemporary works from Wilde's *Salomé* to Thomas Mann's *Gladius Dei* and *Fiorenza*—makes the choice of period less arbitrary than it would otherwise appear.

The setting of the next playlet is precisely dated only because it hinges on a historical event, the death of Titian in 1576; but, as it stands, this fragment is an aesthetic idyll in dialogue form, seemingly incapable of dramatic development because entirely lacking in conflict. The aged painter's last illness serves as a pretext for lyrical reflections on the beauty of landscape and art, on youth and old age, life, dream, and death. Much more than in *Gestern* or any other of the verse plays, one is conscious of the anachronism of the setting and characters. One can imagine these languorous, slightly hermaphroditic youths and maidens as part of the entourage of Beardsley, Böcklin, or Klimt, never of so robust an artist as Titian; or, more easily still, as members of Stefan George's circle, much given, as it was, to archaic fancy dress —and *Der Tod des Tizian* (1892) did, in fact, appear in George's *Blätter für die Kunst*. Yet, in a letter written shortly before his death, Hofmannsthal explained that his work on the play was cut short by his matriculation in the summer of 1892, and that he had planned to confront his characters with the plague; the missing conflicts were to be introduced with a vengeance. Unfortunately Hofmannsthal neither returned to this plan nor gave any indication of it in the many later editions. It was the fame of this fragment, the least characteristic of Hofmannsthal's early works, that gave rise to the total misapprehension of his aims. George, not Hofmannsthal, based all his early activities on the division of human beings into "us" and "the others," the division made by Desiderio in a well-known lyrical passage of the play, an elaboration of a poem that Hofmannsthal wrote in 1890:

Siehst du die Stadt, wie jetzt sie drunten ruht?
Gehüllt in Duft und goldne Abendglut
Und rosig helles Gelb und helles Grau,
Zu ihren Füssen schwarzer Schatten Blau,
In Schönheit lockend, feuchtverklärter Reinheit?
Allein in diesem Duft, dem ahnungsvollen,
Da wohnt die Hässlichkeit und die Gemeinheit,
Und bei den Tieren wohnen dort die Tollen;
Und was die Ferne weise dir verhüllt,
Ist ekelhaft und trüb und schal erfüllt
Von Wesen, die die Schönheit nicht erkennen
Und ihre Welt mit unsren Worten nennen . . .
Denn unsre Wonne oder unsre Pein
Hat mit der ihren nur das Wort gemein . . .
Und liegen wir in tiefem Schlaf befangen,
So gleicht der unsre ihrem Schlafe nicht:
Da schlafen Purpurblüten, goldne Schlangen,
Da schläft ein Berg, in dem Titanen hämmern—
Sie aber schlafen, wie die Austern dämmern.

(Calm lies the city; do you see her now?
Wrapped in her balm and golden evening glow
And rosy lucent yellows, lucent greys,
Blue of black shadows in deep alley-ways?
Her luring beauty, purity veiled in mist?
Yet in this fragrance fraught with premonitions
Vulgarity and ugliness exist,
The mad share lodgings with the brutish there;
And what the distance wisely has concealed
From you is loathsome, dully, drably filled
With creatures of all beauty unaware;

Who yet to designate their world will borrow
The words we use . . . for only words we share
When we or they speak of "our joy," "our sorrow". . .
And though immersed in deepest sleep we lie
Our sleep from theirs still differs utterly:
Here crimson flowers are sleeping, golden snakes,
This hill, asleep, with hammering Titan's quakes—
They sleep much as the oysters live and die.)

Hofmannsthal's contemporary readers could not know
that this speech foreshadows the linguistic crisis which Hofmannsthal was to resolve in favour less of the "we" than of
the "they"; that it is a classical statement of the dilemma of
pre-existence, confined by its own limitations to the beauty
"on the verge of things"; or that the aesthete's awareness of
the "mad and brutish" almost inevitably turns to fascination,
as Rilke was to show in his poems of self-identification with
them in his *Buch der Bilder,* and Hofmannsthal in his story
of the merchant's son. Despite the evidence of Claudio's
opening soliloquy in *Der Tor und der Tod (Death and the
Fool)*—so closely and obviously akin to it—they read Desiderio's speech as though Hofmannsthal had been wholly on
the side of the young artists on the terrace of Titian's villa, of
which Antonio goes on to say:

> *Darum umgeben Gitter, hohe, schlanke,*
> *Den Garten, den der Meister liess erbauen,*
> *Darum durch üppig blumendes Geranke*
> *Soll man das Aussen ahnen mehr als schauen.*

(And that is why these railings, tall and fine,
Surround the park—the Master's own design,
And through lush-blossoming creepers trained between
The world without is guessed at more than seen.)

The overt irony is that Desiderio and Antonio do look
down at Venice, and that their pre-existence is related to life

outside, if only by a loathing more ambiguous than they say. What is more, Hofmannsthal's projected continuation of the play would have lent an almost macabre irony to Desiderio's lines on the fragrance and purity of the distant city—the kind of irony that pervades *Gestern* and *Der weisse Fächer* (1897), only more bitter. Whether or not he intended all these implications when he wrote the lines, very soon it was to be Hofmannsthal who was reprimanded for not keeping on the right side of the railings. In 1896 he asked Stefan George to meet an Austrian friend, Count Joseph Schönborn, who was travelling in Germany and wished to make the Master's acquaintance, though not himself an artist. George replied: "You write a sentence, my dear friend: 'he belongs to life, not to any of the arts,' which I would almost regard as a blasphemy. If a man belongs to no art, has he the right to claim that he belongs to life at all? What? At the most in semi-barbaric ages." This is the very attitude to which Hofmannsthal came to attribute the semi-barbarism of his own age.

As I have already suggested, Hofmannsthal's critique of aestheticism and of the hedonism that was its practical counterpart would be no less outmoded than contemporary tracts like Max Nordau's once-celebrated book if he had not been drawn to these creeds as strongly as he was repelled by them, or if he had not presented them poetically—that is, sympathetically, exhaustively, and in the round. Titian, who never appears in the fragment, is credited with the power to "create life" and to endow both the dreams and the waking perceptions of his pupils with the beauty lent to them by his soul; he is nothing less than a god, the god of the aesthetes. The near-blasphemy committed by Hofmannsthal in his letter to George was a blasphemy against this god, whose High Priest, if not whose very incarnation, George felt himself to be. That Titian should also be mortal, and that Hofmannsthal should have chosen the time of his death, are other implicit ironies which were to become more explicit in his next play, *Death and the Fool.*

The theme of *Gestern*—a lighter playlet that owes something to Musset's *comédies-proverbes,* as well as a great deal to Goethe's *Faust*—also illuminates these ironies. Andrea, its hero, is a practical aesthete; like the many adventurer and adventuress figures in Hofmannsthal's later plays, he believes in living in and for the moment, out of a scepticism close to nihilism:

> *Ohnmächtig sind die Taten, leer die Worte!*
> *Ergründen macht Empfinden unerträglich . . .*

> (Actions are impotent, and words are empty!
> Experience probed becomes unbearable . . .)

It is a vitalism begotten by despair, whose literary history is too long and tedious to be traced here. Once again words are called in doubt, as well as deeds. What is substituted for both is a Bergsonian continuum of activity and sensation, experience for the sake of experience, "life" for the sake of "life" as an escape from time and from the knowledge of an ultimate meaninglessness. That is why experience must not be probed—it had been probed out of existence by a long succession of literary auto-analysts. Hofmannsthal's horror of introversion was a horror of this void.

"Yesterday lies, and only today is true," Andrea asserts, at the beginning of *Gestern.* He is converted not by Death, like Claudio, or by the plague, but by the brief infidelity of Arlette. Though he can understand and forgive her whim in itself, as he is bound to do in the light of his own creed, the continuum of sensation is broken by her single act, and the continuum of time asserts itself. The true nature of time is that it is unredeemable; yesterday and today are no longer opposed, for the past has encroached on the present. Andrea learns that

> *Was einmal war, das lebt auch ewig fort.*

(What once has been lives on eternally.)

The point is made a little blatantly, perhaps—Hofmannsthal was seventeen when he published the play—but it is made in terms of Andrea's own feelings and attitudes, not of a superimposed ethical code. Nor does Hofmannsthal use the machinery of the morality play to make the point, not even the moralizing prologue and epilogue of later playlets. Yet Andrea's condition is very close to Claudio's in *Death and the Fool;* the dividing line between comedy and tragedy is as thin in Hofmannsthal's early work as in Goethe's *Faust,* from which both plays derive. Claudio's pre-existence, like Andrea's, is characterized by a false relationship to time, and thus to reality. If Andrea initiates the succession of Hofmannsthal's adventurers, Faustian mystics of the moment, Casanova-like lyricists of the flesh, then Claudio is the man without a shadow, the potential man incapable of crossing the threshold into reality. Both resemble the Faust of the opening scenes of Part One of Goethe's play in their cult of sensation, their "word-scepticism," and their vain endeavours to become involved in life without committing themselves to temporal ties. That Claudio needs Death—a personified Death—to convert him, and that the claustrophobic mood and the prosody of this play recall the study scenes of *Faust,* does not make it more tragic, or even more serious, than *Gestern.* Andrea's conversion, too, has a counterpart in the Gretchen crisis of *Faust;* and the personification of death in the later playlet tends to turn the whole action into an allegory of an inward process, so that one can almost expect

Claudio to begin a new life when the curtain has fallen.

It may be that Goethe's play helped Hofmannsthal to crystallize his intuitive sense of the connection between the introverted and extroverted aesthete, the pseudo-mystic and the adventurer; but encyclopaedically as he borrowed from the literature and painting of the past, he borrowed what he could afford. The early nineteenth-century setting of *Death and the Fool* serves to veil, not to neutralize, the personal and topical urgency of the problem; and if we are tempted to dismiss the problem itself as a "literary" one, a little reflection will show that it was Hofmannsthal's outstanding achievement to have found the missing link between literary and existential problems in his time. The connection between the aesthete and the adventurer is one instance; a contemporary figure like D'Annunzio—whom Hofmannsthal knew and admired, though not without misgivings—was to show that the two can combine in a single individual. I have said that Claudio's predicament is that of the aesthete, but the aesthete is not necessarily an artist, and the artist is not necessarily an aesthete. Claudio's predicament can be understood in many different ways; amongst other things, he is a psychological type, a case of over-specialization, partial hypertrophy and partial atrophy. Hofmannsthal's ethic, in fact, is the ethic of integration: the integration of body and spirit, feeling and intellect, contemplation and action, the individual and the social man.

To a reader apt to equate morality with puritanism, it might even seem that the moral of *Gestern, Death and the Fool,* and *The Emperor and the Witch* is contradicted by that of *Der weisse Fächer.* Fortunio and Miranda in this playlet seem to stand for the very commitment to time against which Andrea, Claudio, and the Emperor offend. Their fidelity to their dead spouses, however, is a conventional fixation, not a choice embraced by the whole of their natures. What they are faithful to is not enough; they are too young, and their married life was too brief, to have established a continuum of time and experience that could sustain them for the rest of their lives. It is made clear that the love between Fortunio and Miranda has deeper roots in the past than their love for those whom they married; their faithfulness to the dead is as much an escape from reality as the unfaithfulness of Claudio, the hedonism of Andrea, or the Emperor's sensual addiction. Fortunio's widowed grandmother is introduced as a foil to Fortunio's pre-existence; she proves to him that he knows as little about death as about life when he mistakes the cry of a young rabbit killed by a weasel for the cry of a bird. As in the poem *Der Jüngling und die Spinne,* the animal world provides a corrective. To the grandmother, who has known true bereavement and pain, Fortunio is "like an actor who makes up his own part as he goes along, and pays no attention to any cue"; and this autonomy constitutes pre-existence. The paradox of a fidelity that is a kind of infidelity is bound up with a paradox present in the whole of Hofmannsthal's work, that we cannot be truly ourselves till we know how little of our selves is authentically our own. Miranda's conversion, like Fortunio's, springs from her discovery of the outside world; and because her conversion entails an acceptance of the nature of time, the most featherweight of all Hofmannsthal's early playlets comes close to tragedy at this point:

> *morgen aber kommt*
> *Die Sonne, und vor ihr her läuft ein Wind*
> *Und trocknet alles.*
> *Trocken sind die Finger!*
> *Welch eine Welt ist dies, wo böse Zeichen*
> *So schnell zu bannen sind?*

(but tomorrow comes
The sun, and ahead of it runs a wind
And dries all things.
      The dew on my hands has dried!
O what a world is this, where evil omens
Can be so quickly banished?)

The mundane figure of the grandmother and the deliberate casualness with which the problem is posed relate this playlet to *Gestern* and the social comedies of later years, rather than to the most unsocial of all Hofmannsthal's plays, *Das kleine Welttheater* (*The Little Theatre of the World*) of the same year. In this work Hofmannsthal's pre-existence reached its culmination. The sub-title underlines the ecstasy which he experienced in that "glorious but dangerous state," whose climax in the play is the Madman's self-destructive frenzy. Despite the reservation that enabled Hofmannsthal to leave this state behind, and to go on writing when he had done so, this one work of his does almost permit comparison with the visionary poetry of Rimbaud. No one who knew Hofmannsthal's social self would have called him a "mystique à l'état sauvage," as Claudel called Rimbaud, but what makes Hofmannsthal more puzzling than any other great poet of his time is that this highly civilized and seemingly mundane figure contained just such a barbarous visionary. In a letter of 1918 to Rudolf Pannwitz, Hofmannsthal admitted that there was something almost monstrous about his ambition to encompass so much of history and of the human mind. He writes of "the really half naïve, but—if you look at its bad side—terribly arrogant, inmost tendency of my productive nature, towards this aim: to produce out of oneself a whole theatre, a whole repertory. Curiously Viennese, that —it is only lately that I've come to understand this myself." In the same correspondence, he admits "the bizarrerie of my nature generally." When Pannwitz criticized him for sacrificing too much of his individuality to social conventions, and becoming divorced from "the dionysian, ultimately productive" part of himself, Hofmannsthal went so far as to confess that his relation to society was "a much more nihilistic one than you may assume."

To co-ordinate his savagely primitive and his moral visions proved too much for Hofmannsthal at times. A series of dramatic projects that occupied him mainly between 1900 and 1904—the themes were Leda and the Swan, Jupiter and Semele, The Sons of Fortunatus, King Candaules, Pentheus, and Semiramis—are evidence of that element of "I-suppression" which Hermann Broch stressed in his interpretation of Hofmannsthal's development. The conception of all these abandoned works was more "dionysian," more daring in its confrontation of subconscious impulse than the completed works of even this period, the tragedies *Elektra* (1904) and *Ödipus und die Sphinx* (1906). It was in this tragic phase, between his pre-existence and the first of his prose comedies, that Hofmannsthal came closest to Freudian psychology.

Three transitional works are included in the present volume. *Das Bergwerk zu Falun* (*The Mine at Falun*) was a belated attempt on Hofmannsthal's part to return to the imaginative world of his pre-existence. Though he completed this play, only the first of its five acts is included here, in accordance with Hofmannsthal's own inclusion of the first act only among his lyrical plays. His dissatisfaction with the subsequent acts has to do with the theme, rather than the execution. Though the plot derived from a real event, it had been the subject of a tale by the Romantic writer E. T. A. Hoffmann, as well as of a more sober anecdote by J. P. Hebel. By the time he wrote the play, Hofmannsthal would

have liked to reverse the implications of the story itself by
liberating Elis from the pseudo-mystical cravings which Hofmannsthal had come to regard not romantically, but patho-
logically, as an extreme case of introversion and sub-conscious
obsession; but every one of the sources, including the real
event, demanded that Elis should fail in his attempt to marry
and to come to terms with the outside world. It was only in
Die Frau ohne Schatten, as Hofmannsthal remarked in *Ad
me Ipsum,* that he succeeded in "reversing the theme of *The
Emperor and the Witch* and the *Mine:* the love for a daemon
is transmuted into love for a human being, instead of appear-
ing as its antithesis." In this dilemma, too, Hofmannsthal
was not alone; Yeats's play *The Shadowy Waters,* begun at
about the same time but not completed to his satisfaction till
1911, presents a parallel so uncannily close that one is
tempted to attribute both plays to the workings of an international *Zeitgeist.* Even in diction and syntax, Yeats's introduc-
tory lines to his play could have served for Hofmannsthal's:

> I had not eyes like those enchanted eyes,
> Yet dreamed that beings happier than men
> Moved round me in the shadows, and at night
> My dreams were cloven by voices and by fires;
> And the images I have woven in this story . . .
> Moved round me in the voices and the fires.

Yeats's Forgael, too, is a sailor, and he is related to his fellow
sailors in exactly the same way as Hofmannsthal's Elis is to
his, for exactly the same reasons. Forgael says to his com-
panions:

> You've never known, I'd lay a wager on it,
> A melancholy that a cup of wine,
> A lucky battle, or a woman's kiss
> Could not amend.

What sets Forgael and Elis apart is this:

> For it is love that I am seeking for,
> But of a beautiful, unheard-of kind
> That is not in the world.
> > . . . All would be well,
> Could we but give us wholly to the dreams,
> And get into their world that to the sense
> Is shadow . . .
> > . . . Fellow-wanderer,
> Could we but mix ourselves into a dream,
> Not in its image on the mirror!

Even the superficial difference that in Yeats's play it is the shadowy depth of the sea, in Hofmannsthal's the shadowy depth of a subterranean world, that symbolized dream and the subconscious, is suspended at one point of Yeats's play. "And she and I," Forgael says,

> Shall light upon a place in the world's core,
> Where passion grows to be a changeless thing,
> Like charmèd apples made of chrysoprase,
> Or chrysoberyl, or beryl, or chrysolite;
> And there, in juggleries of sight and sense,
> Become one movement, energy, delight . . .

Here Yeats's mineralogy evokes the very setting of Elis' transformation in the mine, just as Peter in Hofmannsthal's play evokes the bottom of the sea in his description of the tavern. A more significant difference is that Yeats managed to keep depth psychology out of his play, whereas Hofmannsthal—whether by design or intuition—went so far as to intimate a kind of mother-fixation on Elis' part; Elis' death-wish, therefore, could be understood as a recognizable symptom, and the mine as a recognizable symbol for pre-existence in a Freudian sense. The same fixation would explain Elis' ultimate failure to marry Anna (in the later acts of the play) and his curiously mixed feelings towards both her and her rival, the Queen of the Mountain. Such Freudian implications occur even in the earlier playlets, such as *The Emperor and the Witch* and *Death and the Fool*. Yeats avoided such implications; but his difficulties over *The Shadowy Waters* were not essentially different from Hofmannsthal's over *The Mine at Falun*. Both had reached a stage in their development at which their Romantic-Symbolist premises were challenged by their own mature experience and by the mental climate of their time. In Hofmannsthal's play the dichotomy is so stark that the realistic and symbolic scenes very nearly fail to fuse into a single action. In Yeats's play, the incongruity is apparent less in the action than in the diction, now colloquial, now erudite as in the mineralogical passage quoted above. Yeats had the obvious advantage of being able to draw on local traditions of supernatural lore, so that those of his characters who stand for the life of the imagination could be related more organically to their opposites; but, unlike Hofmannsthal, he was reluctant to enter sympathetically into the point of view of the pragmatic majority, as he could not help doing if he was to produce drama and sustain the tension on which both his and Hofmannsthal's plays depended. Yeats, one can never doubt for a moment, was on the side of his tragic visionaries, Forgael in *The Shadowy Waters* or Mary in *The Land of Heart's Desire* (1894). Hofmannsthal, on the other hand, would have liked his Elis to embrace the alternative to pre-existence which Maurteen vainly recommends to Mary in the early version of Yeats's play:

> When we are young
> We long to tread a way none trod before,
> But find the excellent old way through love,
> And through the care of children, to the hour
> For bidding Fate and Time and change goodbye.

It has been held against Hofmannsthal that so much of his later commitment seems to be reducible to a commonplace of this order; but so is the commitment of many of those classical authors, such as Molière, whom he most admired. It is true that married love and the care of children assume a mystical significance in several of Hofmannsthal's later works, and that his own sudden death at the age of fifty-five occurred when he was about to leave for the funeral of his eldest son; but married love and the care of children are subjects no more commonplace in themselves than any other. If we consider them drab, it is our own drabness that makes them so. Hofmannsthal's ethic, as I have said, was the ethic of integration; and integration, like other "norms," is a state more easy to talk about than to attain, whether in art or in life. There is a mysticism of common experience, already hinted at in the Smith's speech in Hofmannsthal's *Idylle:*

Die ganze kenn ich, kennend meinen Kreis,
Massloses nicht verlangend, noch begierig ich,
Die flüchtge Flut zu ballen in der hohlen Hand.
Den Bach, der deine Wiege schaukelte, erkennen lern,
Den Nachbarbaum, der dir die Früchte an der Sonne reift
Und dufterfüllten lauen Schatten niedergiesst . . .
Das Haus begreif, in dem du lebst und sterben sollst,
Und dann, ein Wirkender, begreif dich selber ehrfurchtsvoll,
An diesen hast du mehr, als du erfassen kannst—

(I know the whole in knowing my own boundaries,
Not yearning for the immeasurable, nor ever seeking
To clench the fleeting flood within my hollow hand.
The stream which rocked your cradle, that learn to know,
The nearby tree ripening fruit for you in the sun,
Casting down lukewarm shadows heavy with fragrance . . .
Grasp the one house in which you must live and die,
And then, as one accomplishing, grasp your own self with awe;
These things alone are more than ever you'll comprehend.)

This, according to Hofmannsthal, is a more truly religious attitude than the frantic reaching out for the cosmos in pre-existence; yet the tragic alternative, too, is present in his later work, just as the Smith's attitude is implicit in much of his early poetry. The Adventurer and the Gardener are the archetypes of the two modes, and both engaged Hofmannsthal's imagination and sympathy to the end.

Die Hochzeit der Sobeide (*The Marriage of Zobeide*) is the tragedy of a woman who just fails to attain integration through married love. Her tragedy is like that of the merchant's son in Hofmannsthal's earlier story in that her imagination resists her circumstances. The Oriental, Arabian Nights setting of both works has the function of permitting the greatest possible contrast of splendour and squalor, without resort to the supernatural as in *The Emperor and the Witch* or *The Mine at Falun*. Once again it is possible to read the work as a tract against the times—against free love, in this instance, if one chooses to blame the husband's indulgence—but Hofmannsthal's evolution as a dramatist had reached the point where his ethical ends had ceased to clash with his aesthetic means. A shorter and slighter play of 1897, *Die Frau im Fenster,* had exhausted the lyrical possibilities of a related theme, a woman's infidelity that is also a longing for death; there neither the lover nor the husband have an independent existence, for the play is dominated by Dianora's meditations. With the exception of *Der Abenteurer und die Sängerin* of 1898, *The Marriage of Zobeide* was the first of Hofmannsthal's plays to be conceived in terms of drama more than of poetry; and, though he was little more satisfied with it than with *The Mine at Falun,* and considered rewriting it in prose, the flaws in its motivation are outweighed by its tragic force. Tragedy, Hofmannsthal was to discover, was too dynamic, too monomaniacal a medium to permit that complexity of structure, motive, and characterization which distinguished his more realistic plays, from *Der Abenteurer und die Sängerin* onwards. Of all his dramatic works other than librettos and the two morality plays now associated with the Salzburg Festival, it is his comedy *Der Schwierige* (*The Man Who Was Difficult;* 1918) that has established itself most securely on the German and Austrian stage.

Since I have applied the word "realistic" to such works as *Der Schwierige,* I must say again in conclusion that Hofmannsthal never broke with his past in any fundamental regard. "The spirit seeks the real, the nonspirit clings to the unreal," he wrote in his *Book of Friends;* but also: "Naturalism distorts Nature because by copying the surface it has to neglect the wealth of inner relatedness—Nature's real mystery." His later realism could never be more than symbolic, a realism of surfaces only, because he attributed no ultimate reality to the institutions of this world. As the *Prologue to "Antigone"* implies, it was the dreamlike nature of the stage, and the stagelike nature of human life, that fascinated Hofmannsthal, and gave him the strength to grapple till the end of his life with what Yeats cursed as

> plays
> That have to be set up in fifty ways . . .
> Theatre business, management of men,

though he also knew the sheer "fascination of what's difficult." *The Stage as Dream-Image* is the title of one of his essays of 1903; and its theme is the "economy of dreams." What he says there about the theatre holds good for all his later works, whether their setting is contemporary, historical, or mythical. "The man who designs a stage décor must have lived and suffered through his eyes. He must have vowed to himself a thousand times that the visible world alone exists, and he must have asked himself a thousand times with a shudder whether it is not the visible world, of all things, that does *not* exist." The one dramatic subject that occupied Hofmannsthal throughout his working life is that of Calderón's *Life Is a Dream,* the subject on which he based his most ambitious play, *Der Turm* (*The Tower;* 1925 and 1927), the very play into which he put so much of his knowledge of past and present realities, so much of his hopes and fears for the future. Yet Claudio, the closed man of the early play, gives an intimation of this theme of life as a dream play when he dies on the threshold of existence.

Like his creator, the Messianic hero of *The Tower* is the representative of a society that does not exist, never has existed, and will only exist after a revolution not dreamed of in any current political philosophy. That is why Hofmannsthal could confess that, for all his public involvements, his relation to society was "a much more nihilistic one" than it appeared. What demanded his allegiance was not national or cultural institutions as such, but the ideas and principles of which they were the imperfect embodiment. Here again there is no rift between the early work and the later; and it is no less wrong to present the later Hofmannsthal as a conventional defender of the Austrian and European *status quo* —or *status quo ante,* as it had become by the time of his most intense concern with cultural and political issues—than to present Loris as a defender of *fin de siècle* aestheticism. Sigismund in *The Tower* is at once a prince and the lowest of outcasts, condemned to live like a caged animal, and his cause is that of the poor and the oppressed.

The totality of Hofmannsthal's work is as open to misunderstandings as Goethe's. Like Goethe, and unlike most of his contemporaries, he attempted that most difficult thing— difficult enough in Goethe's time, much more in Hofmannsthal's—to extend an essentially personal and esoteric vision to the most diverse spheres, to cut across established divisions and specializations, to make connections everywhere, and produce not only works, but a literature. That Hofmannsthal, as an Austrian, inherited a different culture did not make his task basically different from Goethe's; in trying to produce a literature, "a whole repertory," as he said, he drew not only on a national heritage, but on whatever seemed most congenial to him in ancient, mediaeval, and modern, European and Oriental tradition—Goethe's *Weltliteratur*. Goethe, too. "dabbled" in every branch of literature, including the writing of librettos; nothing was too small for him to attempt, nothing too great. Both denied an ultimate significance to transitory phenomena and institutions, yet applied themselves with intense devotion to their study and service. A century and a half of critical and scholarly industry has not exhausted Goethe's work, or made it widely accessible as a whole, because its diversity is more palpable than its unity. *Mutatis mutandis*—and it is their kind, not their stature, that makes the two writers comparable—the same is likely to be true of Hofmannsthal's work. Every new reading of any one of his works in the light of another reveals new inter-relations, new intricacies of texture and allusion, new seeming contradictions and paradoxes. "Man is a manifold person," Hofmannsthal wrote, and few men were more manifold than he. Because of his unceasing endeavour to grasp and shape this multiplicity, rather than to suppress it for the sake of an easy victory, even his failures remain interesting and admirable.

NOTES

Several previously unpublished notes by Hofmannsthal have been quoted here; they were transcribed from annotated books in Hofmannsthal's library, to which I have had access by kind permission of the poet's son, Mr. Raimund von Hofmannsthal.

The sources for most of the other quotations are named in the text itself, and all the works referred to are to be found in the fifteen-volume edition of Hofmannsthal's works edited by Herbert Steiner and published by S. Fischer Verlag, Frankfurt a/M. Where no such source is mentioned, the quotation is from the diaries and notes included in Volume 15 of the above-named edition. I am grateful to Mr. Rudolf Hirsch, of S. Fischer Verlag, for having read and commented on the text

The letters to the German poet and philosopher Rudolf Pannwitz (b. 1881) from which I have quoted on pp. liv–lv were published by Herbert Steiner in *Mesa* (Lexington, Ky.), autumn 1955. Rudolf Pannwitz's part of the correspondence has not yet been published. The quotation on p. v is based on a transcription made available to me by Hofmannsthal's widow, the late Mrs. Gerty von Hofmannsthal.

The quotations from the *Collected Poems* and *Collected Plays* of W. B. Yeats have been used by permission of Mrs. W. B. Yeats, The Macmillan Company, New York, and Messrs. Macmillan & Co. Ltd., London.

M. H.

The following list gives in alphabetical order the translated titles of works of Hofmannsthal's mentioned in the text:

Der Abenteurer und die Sängerin: The Adventurer and the Singer
Die ägyptische Helena: The Egyptian Helen
Ariadne auf Naxos: Ariadne in Naxos
Die Betrachtungen, die geschnittenen Steine und die redenden Masken: The Reflections, the Cut Stones, and the Speaking Masks
Elektra: Electra
Die Frau im Fenster: The Woman in the Window
Die Frau ohne Schatten: The Woman without a Shadow
Gerechtigkeit: Righteousness
Das gerettete Venedig: Venice Preserv'd
Gespräch über Gedichte: Conversation on Poetry
Gestern: Yesterday
Das grosse Salzburger Welttheater: The Great Salzburg Theatre of the World
Jedermann: Everyman
Der Jüngling und die Spinne: The Youth and the Spider
Das Märchen der 672. Nacht: The Tale of the Six-Hundred-and-Seventy-Second Night
Ödipus and die Sphinx: Oedipus and the Sphinx
Der Schwierige: The Man Who Was Difficult
Der Tod des Tizian: Titian's Death
Der Turm: The Tower
Vor Tag: Before Day
Der weisse Fächer: The White Fan
Weltgeheimnis: World Secret

*

p. 5: All these essays by Loris are more ambiguous than it was possible to elaborate in a brief introduction. Francis Vielé-Griffin's poems, for example, are treated as journalism in verse; this poet, Hofmannsthal says obliquely, "has the very dangerous gift of expressing nearly all those things which he does not feel, and scarcely thinks, with a sophisticated, almost memorable, aptness." Hofmannsthal is critical even of Pater. *"Marius the Epicurean,"* he writes in his essay on Pater of 1894, "demonstrates the inadequacy of any attempt to base one's whole way of life on the aesthetic view."

p. 20:   Ad me Ipsum: Hofmannsthal's private jottings on his own development as an artist; now included in the volume *Aufzeichnungen.*

p. 25:   Freud and Breuer: The *Studies on Hysteria,* which Freud wrote jointly with Josef Breuer more than five years before *The Interpretation of Dreams,* are usually regarded as the starting-point of psychoanalysis.

p. 31:   Bachofen: His *Das Mutterrecht* appeared in 1861. The passage quoted is from the *Gesammelte Werke,* Vol. III (Basel, 1948), p. 823.

p. 34:   ". . . the loveliness/That has long faded . . .": From Yeats's lyric *He Remembers Forgotten Beauty,* in *The Wind among the Reeds* (1899).

PLAYS AND LIBRETTI

PLAYS AND LIBRETTI

I

THOUGH NOT quite twenty-six years old at the turn of the
century, Hofmannsthal had not only come to the end of one
distinct phase, the lyrical, but laid the foundations for the dramatic works of his maturity. His early (1893) adaptation of
the *Alcestis* of Euripides can be regarded as the first of his
strictly dramatic works, and it anticipated his rather different
concern with ancient Greek myths during the early years of the
new century. The extant sketches, of the same year, for a
great mystical and apocalyptic drama based on the life of
Alexander the Great touch on certain themes that he was to
develop thirty years later in *The Tower*. At least one completed
work, *Der Abenteurer und die Sängerin* (1898), had almost succeeded in making the difficult transition from a
drama mainly of monologue to one of delicate interplay
both of character and motif. Together with *The Marriage of
Zobeide,* this play was first performed on the regular stage in
March 1899. Hofmannsthal called both plays "theatre in
verse," as distinct from his earlier "lyrical dramas," and their
performance in the Burgtheater, Vienna, and the
Deutsches Theater, Berlin, marked the beginning of his involvement in "theatre business" proper.

Hofmannsthal's need for active involvement generally
towards the end of his "pre-existence" has already been discussed here in connection with the poems and verse plays. Yet
the peculiar cultural divisions of the time, and the kind of repu-

tation that Hofmannsthal's poetry had won, made the step puzzling—if not positively shocking—to quite a number of his admirers. Nietzsche, whose influence on German intellectuals was pervasive and decisive at this period, had condemned the theatre as "mass art." Stefan George and his Circle upheld Nietzsche's condemnation with a rigour and solemnity that might well have made Nietzsche laugh. Though one of Hofmannsthal's early playlets had appeared in George's *Blätter für die Kunst,* it could pass as a poem in dialogue form and had the further distinction of being both unfinished and utterly unsuitable for the stage. When Hofmannsthal invited George to the first night of his little play *Die Frau im Fenster,* in 1898, he received no direct reply, but a hint after the event that the Circle would soon be making provision for private performances of dramatic works and that this might prove as attractive to Hofmannsthal as "a conventional, inevitably crude presentation on the common boards." George already suspected that it would not. But as a German he could not understand the claustrophobia that would have beset Hofmannsthal if he had acted on the hint.

It was soon after, in 1900, that Hofmannsthal first approached Richard Strauss. Their collaboration was not to begin until 1906, and it happened that at this very time George and the Circle were extending their hostility to the entire art of music. Opera and ballet, in any case, would have been disqualified for their impurities and associations with "mass art"; but now music itself was to be excluded from the civilizing arts, though the dance was saved from total interdiction by its sculptural and corporeal qualities. Much of Hofmannsthal's art as playwright and librettist remained rooted in the same symbolist aesthetic from which George's had sprung; but the externals of hated conventions—of

psychological comedy, for instance, with its seeming concession to the dominant naturalism—were more apparent to
George and his followers than Hofmannsthal's deeper commitment to an art of gesture, mask, and myth. By 1906 Hofmannsthal was beyond the Circle's pale; only its most independent member, Karl Wolfskehl, defied the Master by
keeping in touch with Hofmannsthal in later years.

These circumstances would be trivial if the misunderstanding had been confined to George and his disciples; but
with very few exceptions it was shared by prominent critics of
every school, and it is still apt to crop up in discussions of
Hofmannsthal's libretti. The recent publication in England and America of the correspondence between Richard
Strauss and Hofmannsthal prompted comments that recall
the most blatant misrepresentation of fifty years ago. "We
seem to be watching a Siamese cat working out a *modus
vivendi* with a Labrador," Mr. Edward Sackville-West aptly
remarked in his introduction to the correspondence; and
the personal incompatibility of the two men was even
more extreme than the letters reveal. Thus Mr. Sackville-
West wonders why Hofmannsthal was unwilling to meet the
composer more often than he did. Hofmannsthal's letters
to close friends make it clear that he was less devoted to
Strauss personally than to the work they did together; and
meticulously as he applied himself to anything that concerned the work, he had other commitments and could not
afford to waste time on unnecessary conversations. Count
Harry Kessler mentions in his diary that, after his last meet-
ing with the two men in 1928, Hofmannsthal felt
obliged to apologize to Kessler in writing for the "nonsense"
talked by Strauss. Nor did Hofmannsthal have any illusion about Strauss's merits as a composer; in a letter of
1914 to his friend Bodenhausen he writes that his hair stood

on end when Bodenhausen compared Strauss to Beethoven.

Strauss's much more cordial and uncomplicated relationship to Hofmannsthal, of which Hofmannsthal was well
aware, led several reviewers of the correspondence to come
down heavily on Strauss's side and ascribe Hofmannsthal's
part in the collaboration to various sordid or neurotic motives. That the partnership was successful in many ways,
despite or because of the personal incompatibility, should
have made the critics think again and perhaps even go so
far as to acquaint themselves with some of Hofmannsthal's
non-operatic works. Had he proved less difficult and bizarre
in his collaboration with Richard Strauss than in his independent works, his libretti would not be worth reprinting
and reading for their own sake, and the precarious partnership would be less fascinating and less perplexing than it is.
Hofmannsthal's part in the operas and ballets can be appre-
ciated only in the light of his other works, from the early poetry
to *The Tower*. A number of his libretti—*Ariadne auf
Naxos, Die Frau ohne Schatten*, and *Die ägyptische
Helena*—are sequels, in a more viable medium, to his early
"lyrical dramas." Others are closely akin to the non-operatic
plays of his mature years. Even in retrospect and in the light of
Hofmannsthal's non-operatic works the collaboration appears in no way fortuitous, if only because one can think of
no other composer of the time with whom he might have
worked out a happier or smoother *modus vivendi*. In his review of the correspondence the music critic of *The Times*
(London) complained that Hofmannsthal was a "dyed-in-the-
wool reactionary" and that Strauss "abandoned his forward-
looking traits at the behest of Hofmannsthal"—presuma-
bly because Hofmannsthal repeatedly implored Strauss to
abstain from the "Wagnerian kind of erotic screaming
. . . this shrieking of two creatures in heat" which he found

repulsive, and because he preferred delicate *concertante* effects to mere orchestral volume. If Hofmannsthal's taste in music points to a reactionary disposition, so does the taste of Stravinsky, say, or Bartok, or Hindemith. Without various kinds of primitivism on the one hand and neo-classicism on the other, there would have been precious little "progress" in early twentieth-century music; and both, historically, are regressive trends. Stravinsky has said of his *Pulcinella* adaptation: "It was the epiphany through which all my later work became possible. It was a backward look, of course—the first of my love affairs in that direction—but it was a look in the mirror too." Hofmannsthal's development as a writer was largely a matter of such backward looks that were also "looks in the mirror"; and if he induced Strauss to take a few looks "in that direction," that was all to the good.

Of the distinguished poets of his time, few shared Hofmannsthal's peculiar need for a fusion of words with music, and of the composers that might have been more congenial to him in taste and temperament, none could respond as readily or constantly to this need as Richard Strauss. This simple circumstance explains why Hofmannsthal entered into a partnership which could exasperate him to the point of telling Strauss that it "antagonizes half the world, including even friends I value." These friends were persons towards whom Hofmannsthal could never have been guilty of such bluntness and seeming callousness, just as they would have been incapable of Strauss's injunctions to Hofmannsthal: "So get your Pegasus saddled," or "When composing your text don't think of the music at all—I'll see to that." Somehow or other the Siamese cat had to make an impression on the Labrador; no wonder he was reduced to grotesque and painful antics.

Yet the partnership produced a number of operatic masterpieces. As far as Hofmannsthal was concerned, it involved no sacrifice other than a personal one—and he took care to confine personal relations with Strauss to indispensable meetings. His insistence in the letters on the impersonal nature of the collaboration, which seems priggish at times and gratuitously offensive, rested on deeply held convictions relevant not only to the difference between the two men as men but also as artists. To withhold these convictions from Strauss, or to suspend them for the sake of an easy relationship, would have demanded a sacrifice of integrity. Once again mere hints were not taken; yet if Strauss could not grasp what the idea of impersonality meant to Hofmannsthal, he could not begin to grasp what the libretti were about. To this incomprehension on Strauss's part we owe some of the finest and most revealing letters in the correspondence.

Hofmannsthal's stress on the principle of impersonality in the arts seems to be contradicted by passages in which he calls attention to the importance of his own contribution to the operas and ballets. The particular kind of collaboration that Hofmannsthal wanted—"poetry-*cum*-music," not merely the provision of frames for musical compositions —demanded that Strauss should respond to the poetry and respect its quality. Hofmannsthal was always prepared to make concessions on musical or dramatic grounds—the second act of *The Cavalier of the Rose* is an outstanding instance—but he would not allow Strauss to forget that the two arts must be kept on an equal footing. Self-effacement was one thing, concessions to the composer's literary taste another. If there were occasions when Hofmannsthal had to bring home to Strauss not only that the other art existed in its own right but also that Strauss's librettist had won some distinction in that art, he was driven to the inconsistency by

Strauss's obtuseness and his own exasperation. Considering how long the association lasted, these occasions were rare; and they were counterbalanced by periods of mutual satisfaction and respect.

II

Hofmannsthal's need for "lyrical drama," or melodrama in the strictest sense—that is, for a medium in which words were fused with music—is closely connected with the "word-scepticism" expounded by the fictitious Lord Chandos in his justly famous *Letter;* and Hofmannsthal's so-called Chandos crisis, as already suggested, was not confined to any one period of his life but was anticipated even in the works of that early poetic phase which it is often said to have terminated.

Hofmannsthal's experience of the inadequacy of words —already hinted at in his first verse play, *Gestern* (1891) —involved a whole complex of related matters. Above all, it was inseparable from his awareness of living in a civilization lacking in style, cohesion, and continuity. One of his very first prose pieces, published at the age of seventeen, contains this observation: "We have no generally valid tone in conversation because we have no society and no conversation, just as we have no style and no culture." Hofmannsthal's concern with total art grew out of this dissatisfaction. Art, in this early phase, was the means of creating dreams and illusions powerful enough to banish the barbarous realities of the age. Like much Symbolist doctrine, Hofmannsthal's was based on a stark dualism. Only a fusion of all the arts and their reduction to a common core of expression that was not self-expression alone, but gesture, ritual, and myth, could resist the fragmentation of culture.

In his early essay on Paul Bourget, also published when he was seventeen, Hofmannsthal wrote that in an age of individualism, "no understanding is possible between two persons, no conversation, no connection between today and yesterday" (the theme of *Gestern,* written in the same year); "words lie, feelings lie, even our self-awareness lies." The essay shows the rather Nietzschean addiction at this time to strong sensations, the desire "to feel rushing, living blood: *à sentir sentir";* but when Hofmannsthal writes, "if we can die of the body, we also owe to the body, to the senses, the foundation of all poetry," he is stating a belief which he was to modify, but never wholly renounce. The unity of body and mind is explicitly or implicitly upheld in all the works of his maturity; there are formulations of it in his novel *Andreas* and in his late play *The Tower.* This belief was one basis for Hofmannsthal's aesthetic of gesture. Indeed, the early essay opens up the whole complex of Hofmannsthal's most characteristic preoccupations; from his "word-scepticism"—clearly expressed here ten years before the Chandos Letter—to the questions of individuality and tradition.

Hofmannsthal's interest in the actor and the dancer goes back to the same early period. Both could transcend words, circumstance, and personal identity. Hofmannsthal put it like this in an early tribute to Eleonora Duse, the first of two such tributes written in 1892: "We do not know where the limits of her art might be. Not in individuality, since she has none, or any whatever." In a letter of the same year Hofmannsthal tells his friend that it makes no difference whether he knows Italian well, since Duse "acts the sense, not the words."

It is significant, too, that the so-called Chandos crisis should have been most clearly anticipated in another tribute to an actor, Hofmannsthal's review, in 1895, of a book on Friedrich Mitterwurzer. Here Hofmannsthal remarks:

For people are tired of listening to talk. They feel a deep disgust with words. For words have pushed themselves in front of things. Hearsay has swallowed the world. . . . We are in the grip of a horrible process in which thought is utterly stifled by concepts. Hardly anyone now is capable of being sure in his own mind about what he understands, what he does not understand, of saying what he feels and what he does not feel. This has awakened a desperate love for all those arts which are executed without speech: for music, for the dance, and all the skills of acrobats and jugglers.

Akin to these last is the clown Furlani who plays such an important, though concealed, part in Hofmannsthal's much later comedy *The Difficult Man*.

The actor, like the poet, is a *persona* in the original sense of the word, a mask or mouthpiece through which not one man but all humanity speaks. That is why Hofmannsthal was able to allow him an ideal and archetypal function which most of his predecessors and contemporaries reserved for the dancer; and that is why he could write in his late collection of aphorisms, the *Book of Friends:* "Between the fleeting fame of the actor and the allegedly lasting fame of the poet, there is but a small and specious difference." The full force of that casual remark comes home to one if he imagines how it would have been received by Stefan George, by one of his idolatrous followers, or even by one of Rilke's more devout lady admirers. (Rilke himself could have understood it, and understood that it was aimed not at poetry but at the cult of personalities.)

Hofmannsthal's poems on the deaths of actors are especially revealing in this connection. The earliest was written for the same actor, Mitterwurzer, after his death in 1897;

and it is the question of identity that makes these occasional poems relevant to Hofmannsthal's deepest and
most constant concerns:

> *Er fiel: da fielen alle Puppen hin,*
> *In deren Adern er sein Lebensblut*
> *Gegossen hatte; lautlos starben sie,*
> *Und wo er lag, da lag ein Haufen Leichen,*
> *Wüst hingestreckt: das Knie von einem Säufer*
> *In eines Königs Aug gedrückt, Don Philipp*
> *Mit Caliban als Alp um seinen Hals,*
> *Und jeder tot.*

> *Da wussten wir, wer uns gestorben war:*
> *Der Zauberer, der grosse, grosse Gaukler!*
> *Und aus den Häusern traten wir heraus*
> *Und fingen an zu reden, wer er war.*
> *Wer aber war er, und wer war er nicht?*

> *Er kroch von einer Larve in die andre,*
> *Sprang aus des Vaters in des Sohnes Leib*
> *Und tauschte wie Gewänder die Gestalten.*

(He fell: then all the puppets collapsed with him
Into whose veins he'd poured his own life-blood.
Now speechlessly they died; and where he lay
There also stretched out a heap of corpses
In wreck and ruin: knee of a drunkard
Pressed into a king's eye; Don Philip
With Caliban a nightmare round his neck,
All of them dead.

Then we knew whom death had taken from us:
The sorcerer, the great great conjurer,
And we came from our houses, gathered round
And so began to talk of what he was.
Who was he though, and who else was he not?

68

He crept out of one mask into another,
Sprang from the father's into the son's body
And changed his shape as though it were his clothes.)

Much the same question is posed in the poem *On the Death of the Actor Hermann Müller* (1899), though here Hofmannsthal dwelt more poignantly on the dualism of real and assumed identity, of the dream projected on the stage and the reality from which even actors were not exempt:

> *Doch wenn das Spiel verlosch und sich der Vorhang*
> *Lautlos wie ein geschminktes Augenlid*
> *Vor die erstorbne Zauberhöhle legte*
> *Und er hinaustrat, da war eine Bühne*
> *So vor ihm aufgetan wie ein auf ewig*
> *Schlafloses aufgerissnes Aug, daran*
> *Kein Vorhang je mitleidig niedersinkt:*
> *Die fürchterliche Bühne Wirklichkeit.*
> *Da fielen der Verwandlung Künste alle*
> *Von ihm, und seine arme Seele ging*
> *Ganz hüllenlos und sah aus Kindesaugen.*

> (Yet when the play was fading, and the curtain
> Came down in silence like a painted eyelid
> Over the magic cavern emptied now of life,
> And he stepped out, a stage appeared before him
> Like a wide, sleepless eye for ever open
> On which no curtain mercifully falls,
> The terrifying stage, reality.
> Then all the arts of transformation dropped
> From him, and his poor soul walked quite unclothed
> And gazed from a child's eyes.)

True, this dualism did not detract from the actor's exemplary function, since it was one that Hofmannsthal himself experienced and rendered in all his earlier works.

Yet the Symbolist notion of "the stage as dream image" —the title of an essay by Hofmannsthal published in 1903—

had to be reconciled with reality in some way, much as the ideal of impersonality had to be reconciled with what was valid in personality. The change is apparent in Hofmannsthal's later tributes to actors and in his later writings on the theatre. Hofmannsthal's own dramatic works of the transitional period bridge the gulf in several different ways. The essay on "the stage as dream image" recommends De Quincey, Poe, and Baudelaire as favourite authors of the perfect designer of stage décors; but Hofmannsthal jotted down the draft of a crucial passage of the essay on the back flyleaf of a volume containing Shakespeare's *Macbeth, Hamlet,* and *King Lear.* Hofmannsthal's modification of the Symbolist aesthetic owes a great deal to his study of Shakespeare, of the Greek dramatists whose works he adapted at this time, as well as of Calderón, Molière, and the whole repertory of classical, medieval, and modern drama. It was in his lecture on Shakespeare of 1905 that Hofmannsthal remarked on the "space between characters" that is "not a vacuum but a space mystically alive," and this became such an important element in his own art that he was to coin a new word, "allomatic," to describe the mysterious relationship.

Hofmannsthal began by celebrating the "truth of masks" and of that dream image which the stage opposes to the "terrifying stage, reality." So in his Prologue to the *Antigone* of Sophocles (1899):

> *Die Maske aber darf dich nicht verstören:*
> *es tragen die Geliebtesten der Menschen*
> *vor dir ein maskenhaft Gesicht:*
> *ein menschlich Aug erträgt nichts Wirkliches.*

> (You have no need to let my mask perturb you:
> even the dearest beings that you know,

they only let you see the masks they wear:
the eye of man cannot bear that which is real.)

The masked Spirit of Antigone in this Prologue asserts
that only on the stage there is truth:

alles andre
ist Gleichnis und ein Spiel in einem Spiegel.

(all other things
are parables and playings in a mirror.)

But in 1903 Hofmannsthal began to write his *Jeder-mann*, the first of his plays derived from medieval and Ba-roque dramatic conventions that make the theatre an alle-gory of life. A passage in his *Vorspiel für ein Puppentheater* (1906) marks the significance of the change: "From this dream I rise and step over into that other dream which is called human world and human life." In 1902 Hofmannsthal had also begun that adaptation of Calderón's *Life Is a Dream* which was to occupy him for the rest of his life, gradually turning into his own most personally committed play, *The Tower*. The dualism of dream and reality had be-come far less drastic and far more complex. If life was not as real as it had once seemed, the stage did not need to be as dreamlike as Hofmannsthal had believed; and if per-sonality was not as individual as it had seemed, Hofmanns-thal could now draw closer to the current realistic and social drama. Even psychological comedy, he was soon to discover, could include the wordless gesture, the mystery, and the myth.

In a third article on Eleonora Duse, written in 1903, Hofmannsthal found it necessary to modify his earlier trib-utes to her. Duse had now become greater than the parts she played; she had "suffered the afflictions of our age like no one else, and in a magnificent way"; she had acquired wisdom and become "the embodiment of an un-namable tragic force." Here Hofmannsthal's personal aquaintance with the actress—she was to play the title role in his *Electra,* and Jocasta in his *Ödipus und die Sphinx*—may seem to have involved him in a contradiction; but a diary entry of 1904 points to an inherent paradox that bears on the question of individuality and Hofmannsthal's changing attitude to it. *"Paradox of the Actor:* Duse to-day can impersonate only herself, i.e., in every role she acts the mature woman grown wonderful through love and suffering; i.e., she now raises every role to the universal plane." Personality, Hofmannsthal implies here and elsewhere in his later work, becomes a positive value as soon as it em-braces more than the merely individual and circumstantial.

The same change and the same paradox are evident in the last of Hofmannsthal's poems in memory of actors, that writ-ten on the death of the great actor Josef Kainz, whom Hof-mannsthal had known personally and who had also acted in two of his plays. The manuscript of the poem in the Vienna Nationalbibliothek is dated 2 October 1910. Like the later Duse, and unlike the two other actors commemo-rated in poems by Hofmannsthal, Kainz is seen not only as the vehicle of transformations but as a personality equal to, or greater than, the parts enacted; as

> *Ein Unverwandelter in viel Verwandlungen,*
> *Ein niebezauberter Bezauberer,*
> *Ein Ungerührter, der uns rührte, einer,*
> *Der fern war, da wir meinten, er sei nah . . .*
> *Und Bote eines namenlosen Herrn.*

> (One untransformed in many transformations,
> A great enchanter never himself enchanted,
> A man unmoved who moved us, one
> Who, when we thought him near, was far from us . . .
> Messenger to us of a nameless Lord.)

The allusion to an unexplained mission indicates a kind of personality that is more than individuality. Kainz, in the same poem, becomes the "actor without a mask," and another passage dwells on an aspect of this kind of personality that Hofmannsthal also emphasized in other later writings:

> *O wie das Leben um ihn rang und niemals*
> *Ihn ganz verstricken konnte ins Geheimnis*
> *Wollüstiger Verwandlung! Wie er blieb!*
> *Wie königlich er standhielt!*

> (O how life clutched at him, and never yet
> Could quite ensnare him in the mystery of
> Voluptuous transformation! How he *stayed!*
> How royally he stood fast!)

Hofmannsthal's cult of the actor had its roots in his early intuition that the very word *self* is "little more than a metaphor," and that "we and the world are not different things." This intuition was the source of much of Hofmannsthal's early lyrical poetry and early lyrical drama, though even in these works he was looking for an ethical principle that would prevent this metaphorical self from simply evaporating and would govern its relationship to the here and now. Though the individual could never be autonomous or clearly circumscribed, true personality demanded a commitment not only to the flux of being—"to have genius is to participate in the unreason of the cosmos," Hofmannsthal noted towards the end of his life—but to some fixed point outside the self. This is the constancy or loyalty attributed to Kainz in the poem, though the actual commitment is not explained.

What Hofmannsthal attempted everywhere in his life and works was to combine both these commitments—to be loyal to certain conventions and institutions, yet to remain open to the mystery and the flux. As he wrote in his prologue of 1926 to Brecht's first play *Baal*, "We move within forms and conventions without sacrificing the mystery of life to them," contrasting this attitude with that of the younger generation. In Brecht's play and its "crude inarticulate language" Hofmannsthal saw "the end of individualism . . . that child of the seventeenth century which the nineteenth fattened up"; he both censured and welcomed them as an expression of an amorphous energy, a chaos that might engender a new age.

I do not wish to suggest that Hofmannsthal ever finally unravelled this complex of problems and paradoxes. "The shaped work settles the problem," he wrote, and the verb implies that problems are only "solved" in the abstract. Comparing the mime and the dancer with the actor in his essay *On Pantomime,* Hofmannsthal had written that the former must be "lacking in individuality, which cannot be conveyed in any medium other than language"; yet a diary entry of 1921 reads as follows: "The individual is inexpressible. Whatever is expressed, immediately takes on a general aspect and ceases to be individual in any strict sense. Language and individuality are mutually exclusive." We are left with the paradox and the mystery with which Hofmannsthal had been at grips for thirty years, and with the inference that the individual is inexpressible in any medium whatever. This points to the core of Hofmannsthal's own art—an art of "I"-suppression, Hermann Broch called it—and comes as close as I wish to come to an explanation of Hofmannsthal's cult of the actor, his renunciation of lyrical poetry, and his resort to various mixed media. In the same late prologue to Brecht's play the actor is characterized once more as "the amoeba among living creatures, the indeterminate archetypal creature that lets the situation prescribe whether it is to be animal or vegetable"; and "that is why he is the symbolic man."

The actor's medium, like the poet's, is words, and both

actor and poet are subject to the limitations and responsibilities imposed by that medium; yet both also transcend them: the poet by his capacity to render the timeless moment and transform circumstance into myth, the actor by his capacity to render not the words, but the sense, in pure gesture. It is this latter aspect of the actor that accounts for Hofmannsthal's tendency to speak of actors and dancers as though their function were one and the same.

Hofmannsthal's dance libretti are less well known than his opera libretti, but he wrote quite a number of them—for the traditional ballet, for Diaghilev, and for the solo dancer Grete Wiesenthal, a close personal friend. Dance forms an important part of several of Hofmannsthal's dramatic works, beginning with the climax of his *Electra*. The first work that Hofmannsthal offered to Richard Strauss, in 1900, and well before Strauss's composition of *Electra,* was a ballet libretto, *Der Triumph der Zeit.* This was the first of a long succession of dance libretti and "pantomimes" no less various in setting and style than Hofmannsthal's plays and opera libretti; the last, *Achilles auf Skyros,* was written in 1925.

"Dance," Frank Kermode wrote, "is the most primitive, non-discursive art, offering a pre-scientific image of life, an intuitive truth. Thus it is the emblem of the Romantic image. Dance belongs to a period before the self and the world were divided, and so achieves naturally that 'original unity' which modern poetry can produce only by a great and exhausting effort of fusion." Hofmannsthal's earliest references to dance belong to the brief phase in which he combined a Nietzschean vitalism and primitivism with a taste for the latest refinements of "decadent" art. His second essay on Duse of 1892 speaks of artists as "raising the unconscious to our awareness in words that die away, in fugitive gestures, and immersing it in dionysian beauty." In the same year he praised Swinburne's poems as vessels filled with "darkly glowing, potent wine of life, pressed from grapes from which dionysian ecstasy and anguish and dance and madness well, mysteriously blended." This tribute draws on the international vocabulary of contemporary aestheticism; but even in later years dance retained its associations for Hofmannsthal with orgiastic ecstasy, anguish, and madness. Where he tried to render these in another medium—as in a whole succession of mythical dramas, of which *Pentheus, Leda und der Schwan*, and *Semiramis* are outstanding—he produced only drafts and fragments. Only "fugitive gestures," wordless and "nameless," could convey them.

Yet Hofmannsthal's essays and his dialogue *Fear*—a work closely akin to Paul Valéry's *L'Âme et la danse*, but written some fifteen years earlier—at least evoke such moments in words, in a rhythmic and vivid prose peculiar to his visions of primitive mysteries. So in his *Dialogue on Poems* of 1903, mainly a tribute to Stefan George's works, which contains this passage on the ancient wine press:

Those who press the grapes feel like gods. They feel as though Bacchus were right in their midst while they work by night. As though he were stamping beside them, his long robe gathered up to above the knee, in the red juice whose very vapour intoxicates. They are at once bathers and dancers: and it is the drunkenness of their dancing that makes their bath rise higher and higher. The new wine gushes from the press in streams; like little ships the wooden cups sway on the purple flood. . . . In the vapoury darkness, amid screams, amid swaying torchlight, and the splashing of the blood of the grapes, suddenly Aphrodite is born from the purple foam: Bacchus rose from the wine-press, wild as a leaping wave, and drenched a garment, so that it flowed down like a shining nakedness, and out of a girl he created the goddess around whose body desire and rapture flow.

Fear (1907) is a dialogue between two Greek dancing girls, Laidion and Hymnis. Its theme is Hofmannsthal's constant concern with the trammels of individuality and the casting off of those trammels in art. Laidion suggests to Hymnis that all their impersonations and transformations in the dance are incomplete because they can never wholly escape from personal desire, from hope, and its concomitant fear. Laidion is obsessed by the thought of a barbarian island community whose dancing is impersonal because it is an annual rite, not a professional skill. Its women are "virgins and have forgotten it, they are to become women and mothers and have forgotten it: to them everything is ineffable. And then they dance."

At this point in the dialogue words fail Laidion: "She begins to sway from the hips. Somehow one feels that she is not alone, that many of her kind are around her and that all are dancing at once under the eyes of their gods. They dance and circle as dusk falls: shadows detach themselves from the trees and sink down into the crowd of dancers, and out of the tree-tops rise great birds housing the departed spirits, and join the circle, and beneath them all the island vibrates like a boat filled with drunken people. . . ."

Laidion has only heard about the island from a sailor; and the element of doubt as to whether there really is, or ever has been, a place where women could be "happy without hope," that is, wholly divested of their personal desires and fears, is an ironic reflection on the literary cult of the dancer in Hofmannsthal's time. Yet clearly the dancer was less subject to those complications and paradoxes which beset Hofmannsthal's cult of the actor as "symbolic man." Hofmannsthal's essay on Oscar Wilde of 1905, itself the celebration of a myth, concludes with a quotation from the Persian that sums up the peculiar mystery which Hofmannsthal attributed to the dance: "He who knows the power of the dance of life fears not death. For he knows that love kills." Hofmannsthal's Electra alludes to the same mystery.

At the same period, in 1906, Hofmannsthal wrote a tribute

to Ruth St. Denis, who became a personal friend and visited him at Rodaun the following year. Hofmannsthal's letters of these years confirm the deep impression made on him by "the incomparable dancer," as the title of the essay calls her. After discussing the influence of the East on Ruth St. Denis's art and on contemporary Europe generally—but with the reservation that "a whole youth, immersed in the dream of the East, or the intuition of a second, the glimpse of a single temple dancer, a single image, may have condensed into these unforgettable gestures, these dances"—Hofmannsthal continues: "Yet I shall hardly attempt to describe her dancing. Whatever one could describe in a dance would never be more than the incidentals: the costume, the sentiment, the allegory. Here nothing is sentimental, nothing allegorical, and even the costume, that glittering drapery which amid the enchantment of rhythmic, gradually intensifying movements suddenly yields to sudden nudity, the vision of which is rendered mysterious by the strange colouring of the light, and grave, severe as the vision of an undraped sacred statue in the enclosed space of a temple—this costume embroidered with gold (or whatever else she might wear on other occasions) is of incomparably small importance."

Hofmannsthal dwells on the dancer's smile, comparing it to that enigmatic smile which fascinated generations of writers after Pater, and which Hofmannsthal had already invoked in his early verse play *Death and the Fool*—"a mysterious smile always present in her motionless eyes: the smile of a Buddha statue. A smile not of this world. An absolutely unfeminine smile. A smile somehow related to the impenetrable smile in pictures by Leonardo. A smile that attracts the souls of uncommon persons and, from the first moment, but lastingly, alienates the hearts of women and the sensual curiosity of very many men. —And now the dance begins. It consists of movements. It consists of movements that merge with the next in an unceasing rhythmic flow. It is the same as what one saw the little Javanese girls dance in Paris in 1889, and this year the dancers of the King of Cambodia. Naturally it is the same thing to which all oriental dancers aspire; to the dance itself, the essential dance, the silent music of the human body. A rhythmic flow of incessant, and, as Rodin says, of right movements."

Hofmannsthal then praises "the incredible immediacy of what she does, that severe, almost rebuffing immediacy" which makes Isidora Duncan seem like a "professor of archeology" in comparison with "this Lydian dancer who has stepped down from the relief." Yeats and Valéry would have seen the point of this tribute; it is in the tradition which Frank Kermode has recorded in *Romantic Image* and in his postscript to it, the essay quoted above.

A shorter appreciation of Nijinsky's performance in *L'Après-Midi d'un Faune*—the poem which Stefan George had copied in his hand from Mallarmé's manuscript and presented to Hofmannsthal—was published in 1912. Like Duse and Kainz, Nijinsky fitted into no scheme; he was no simple dancer, but "something between the producer, the performer, and the inventor, uniting all three functions in one person." Hofmannsthal's remark that both the poem and the music are in a sense subordinated to Nijinsky's original creation, and his stress on the concentration, economy, and "density of texture" that distinguish Nijinsky's art, are tributes to the dancer's active and positive personality; but Hofmannsthal's choice of the word "pantomime" to describe this dance, and his comparison of it once more with classical sculpture, relate even this exceptional phenomenon to the idea of a total art that renders the inexpressible.

The Austrian dancer Grete Wiesenthal was trained for the ballet. Mainly under the impact of seeing Isidora Duncan dance in Vienna, and with the help of the painters Rudolf Huber and Erwin Lang, she developed her own kind of "expressive" solo or group dancing—the latter together with her sisters. Her autobiography, *Die Ersten Schritte,* touches on her association with Hofmannsthal, of which she writes in a letter: "Hugo von Hofmannsthal was truly interested in, and receptive to, the art of dance—and so, beside Gustav Mahler and Alfred Roller, he was one of the first to recognize my kind of dancing and give it his support. It was just at the time when my sisters and I turned away from the so-called classical ballet, which had become rigid and lifeless, and we were allowed to infuse the dance with new life and vigour. And that is how the pantomime *Das Fremde Mädchen,* a work by Hugo von Hofmannsthal which he wrote for me, came to be performed; the same pantomime was later filmed as well." Hofmannsthal had written another dance libretto, *Amor and Psyche,* for Grete Wiesenthal, in 1911, and he published the two works in a separate volume, together with his dialogue *Fear,* his essay *On Pantomime* and related writings by Goethe and Chuang-Tsu. The later libretto, *Das Fremde Mädchen,* is remarkable for its realistic setting and the fascination for a rich young man of a squalid, criminal underworld—a theme that had preoccupied Hofmannsthal ever since his first story of 1894, *The Tale of the 672nd Night,* and his poems and verse plays of the same early period.

Hofmannsthal's essay *On Pantomime* (1911) is the most comprehensive and illuminating of all his writings on the actor and the dancer, not least because it subsumes both figures and reduces both arts to their common element of gesture. "A pure gesture is like a pure thought that has been stripped even of the momentarily witty, the restrictedly individual, the grotesquely characteristic," Hofmannsthal writes, and goes on to distinguish all these accretions from true personality. In a letter to Carl Burckhardt of 1928 Hofmannsthal outlined the plan of a comedy never completed in which one character, a notorious liar, decides to become a dancer and "says he has chosen this profession because he adores the truth, and dancing is the only profession in which there is *nothing but* truth." This is the truth rendered in gesture, and only in gesture or in pre-articulate thought. The essay continues:

In pure thought, personality appears by virtue of its nobility and strength, though not in a way perceptible at once to everyone. So too in pure gestures the true personality comes to light, and the renunciation of individuality is more than amply compensated. We see a human body that moves in a rhythmic flow, in response to infinite modulations prescribed by an inner genius. It is a man like ourselves who moves before us, but more freely than we ever move, and yet the purity and freedom of his gestures convey exactly what we want to convey when, inhibited and spasmodically, we discharge our inner plenitude. But is it only the freedom of the body that delights us here? Does not the soul reveal itself here in a special way? Does it not discharge its inner plenitude as in music, but more immediately still, with greater concentration? Words arouse a sharper sympathy, but it is vicarious, as it were, intellectualized, generalized; music, a more intense sympathy, but it is vague, longingly digressing; that evoked by gesture is clear and all-embracing, vividly present, joy-giving. The language of words is seemingly individual, but in truth generic; that of the body is seemingly general, but in truth highly personal. Nor is it body that speaks to body, but the human whole that speaks to the whole.

The painter, the sculptor, the architect, the composer, the juggler, and the clown—these are a few of the figures who would have to be related to those of the actor and the dancer to make this survey complete. Hofmannsthal's concern with style extended to crafts and pastimes, to furniture and utensils, to gardens—in which he saw a symbol of all art—and to the minutiae of social convention. His writings on the visual arts, including architecture, are as perceptive as those on literature, the theatre, and the dance, and as rich in those moments of vision which make his essays an essential part of his imaginative work.

Gesture supports, or takes over from, words at critical moments in Hofmannsthal's plays and opera libretti; and his "word-scepticism" pervades their motivation and dialogue. One instance is the Casanova-like figure Florindo in his comedy *Cristinas Heimreise,* of whom one could say that he makes love to women out of an extreme reluctance to talk to them. "Words are good," he says, "but there's something better." (He seizes her hand.) "I don't want to turn this thing into talk." The Captain, Florindo's opposite in other respects, shares the conviction that "with us, all that is finest and most beautiful lies between words." And there is a gloss on this comedy in Hofmannsthal's prose piece *Ways and Encounters* (1907), where he writes: "Not the embrace, it seems to me, but the encounter is the truly decisive erotic pantomime," because "the encounter promises more than the embrace can keep," and "at no moment sensuality is so soulful or soulfulness so sensual as in the encounter." This is Hofmannsthal's philosophy of gesture on another plane. The gesture celebrates a moment—and more than a whole lifetime can contain; it is fugitive and timeless. Such moments and gestures recur throughout his plays and libretti; and everywhere they are dialectically contrasted with that sense of continuity, that loyalty to a single moment of commitment which Florindo lacks and the Captain possesses, despite his adventurous past. Florindo is merely a "word-sceptic"; the Captain is a "word-mystic" as well.

The reference to music in the essay *On Pantomime* suggests that Hofmannsthal thought less well of, and had thought less deeply about, this art than about acting, dancing, or the visual arts; and it is true that Hofmannsthal was primarily what the Germans call an *Augenmensch,* a man more receptive to visual than to auditive impressions. In an early postcard to Marie Herzfeld, accepting an invitation to listen to piano music in her house, Hofmannsthal added: "But I know nothing at all about music, and don't like people who talk about it cleverly—evidently, because I can't do so myself." Since Hofmannsthal could talk very cleverly about literature and the visual arts even in his adolescence, this admission is of some interest. "I am really unmusical," he admitted to Strauss as late as 1923; but the correspondence itself and scattered references to music and composers elsewhere show that his taste and interest in music developed in later years.

The sympathy aroused by music, Hofmannsthal writes in the essay, is "vague, longingly digressing"; though he may have had Romantic music in mind here—and it was the heavily Romantic tendencies in Strauss's music of which he least approved—the remark is generally valid in that music is a progressive art, dependent on duration in time. What Hofmannsthal feared in his collaboration with Strauss is that the moment and the gesture might be lost in a continuum of sound (if not in a continuum of noise, such as the Wagnerian "erotic screaming" which Hofmannsthal found brutish and revolting). Nothing is more telling in this regard than Hofmannsthal's letter to Strauss of 1911 about the staging of

Ariadne auf Naxos, the most delicately lyrical of all his libretti:

Even if I think . . . only of the two groups, Ariadne-Bacchus, Zerbinetta and the four men—even then I must tell myself that they need a mysterious power higher than music alone in order to reveal their ultimate significance at all. The subtly conceived exiguity of this play, these two groups acting beside each other in the narrowest space, this most careful calculation of each gesture, each step, the whole like a concert and at the same time like a ballet—it will be lost, meaningless, a tattered rag, in incompetent hands; only in Reinhardt's, yours and mine can it grow into a singing flower, the incarnation of dance. *Love* is what it needs, enthusiasm, improvisation. . . .

The operative words here are *gesture, concert, ballet, singing flower, incarnation of dance, love,* and *improvisation.* Music, to Hofmannsthal, was one means of making up for the lyrical poetry he had renounced because it was at once too personal in origin and too difficult to reconcile with the social, conventional functions of language; but music was one means only, and not the most effective at that. It had one obvious advantage over the spoken word, even when combined with it in opera: "Song is marvellous because it tames what otherwise is nothing but the organ of our self-seeking, the human voice." But total, concerted art aimed at the realization of the timeless moment and the pure gesture, and their paradigm was the dance.

III

Electra, the first of Hofmannsthal's works to be set to music by Strauss, was written, published, and performed as a play several years before Strauss started work on the composition. But for this fact, which is sometimes overlooked, it might well seem as though Hofmannsthal had deliberately set out to provide Strauss with the kind of text best fitted to succeed Wilde's *Salomé*. Hofmannsthal's play, however, was one of a number on Greek subjects which he planned or executed at this period, the period of his Chandos Letter and his renunciation of lyrical poetry. It was followed by *Ödipus und die Sphinx* (1905) and an adaptation of the *Oedipus Rex* of Sophocles (1906). Hofmannsthal intended to complement *Electra* with a play devoted to Orestes, but abandoned this project, like other fascinating explorations of ancient myths preserved in sketches for a *Leda und der Schwan* (1900–1904), *Jupiter und Semele* (1901), and *Pentheus* (1904). These sketches are illuminating because they show how close Hofmannsthal came in these years to the chthonic regions rediscovered by Nietzsche and Bachofen, to Dionysian mysteries and magical cults. Hofmannsthal's concern, at the same time, with the new depth psychology does much to explain why he was defeated by several of these subjects. Thus Pentheus is described as a "mystic who is sometimes assailed by the horrifying suspicion that he may be a sceptic," much as Hofmannsthal was to describe his Lord Chandos as "a mystic without a mystique"; and there is a symbolic motif that turns out to be symbolic of the subconscious: "that Pentheus does not know his own palace: does not know the grotto, nor the subterranean ponds, nor yet the shaft that leads into the mountain by a trap door (it is near this that he stands later, crying into it: Mother, Mother!)." A similarly ambiguous symbolism had already crept into Hofmannsthal's earlier verse play *The Mine at Falun;* but the sketches openly allude to "pathology, criminal psychology," to "phallic exuberance" and to a "chthonic god" whom the women go out to worship. The supernatural is related to the bestial. In *Jupiter und Semele* Hofmannsthal

85

is also concerned with a "mysterious Queen" figure, akin to that in *The Mine at Falun,* whom he had encountered in Mabel Collins' theosophical romance *The Idyll of the White Lotus;* significantly he identifies her with the Muse. The sketches for *Jupiter und Semele* contain this revealing dictum: "The true domain of the poet: the relation of mind to body, of idea to expression, of man to beast."

Electra, too, appears to have its being in this domain, to the exclusion of all those concerns which unify Hofmannsthal's works of earlier and later periods. One critic, the late E. M. Butler, described the play as a "Graeco-Freudian myth," and quoted an interesting passage in a book by Hofmannsthal's friend Hermann Bahr. In this book, exactly contemporary with Hofmannsthal's *Electra,* Bahr drew attention to the "hysteria" that beset the whole of Greek culture, and claimed that "tragedy, in fact, aims at nothing other than what those two physicians [Freud and Breuer] do: it reminds a people made ill by its culture of what it does not wish to be reminded of, the bad impulses which it conceals. . . ." Hofmannsthal's library does, in fact, contain first editions of Breuer's and Freud's *Studies in Hysteria* (1895) and of Freud's *The Interpretation of Dreams* (1900); yet to call *Electra* a "Graeco-Freudian myth" is to forget that poets have always had access to the domain in question, and that Freud, at the most, was one of Hofmannsthal's many diverse guides to it. E. M. Butler's distaste for Freudian psychology led her to a sweeping judgment on *Electra* generally: "Just as disturbing to Hofmannsthal's native genius was his preoccupation with Greek tragedy. It transformed him temporarily from a delicate, subtle poet who dealt in shades and pastel tints and lilting lyrics into a frenzied creator of turgid spiritual melodrama, whose findings remain extremely questionable, and against which one instinctively rebels." But

Electra contains many subtleties and pastel tints that escaped E. M. Butler's attention in her concentration on its Freudian aspects. She draws attention to Electra's analysis of her mother's dreams and fantasies, but not to the supremely ironic function of this quasi-Freudian treatment in the play as a whole; and she shows no awareness of all the metaphysical and mystical strands—very much in evidence, too, in Hofmannsthal's "lilting lyrics"—that are interwoven with the imagery of "birth, copulation, and death."

Nor is *Electra* as remote from Hofmannsthal's earlier and later works as it may seem. The tendency at present is to follow Hofmannsthal himself in stressing its affinity with all those plays in which he tried to transcend the self-centered and introverted mysticism of his "pre-existence." In *Ad me Ipsum* he writes of "the way to life and to men through sacrifice: two myths: Alcestis and Oedipus. Sacrifice as self-renunciation." And again: "The way to the social as the way to one's higher self: the non-mystical way: (a) through the deed; (b) through the work; (c) through the child . . . (a): transformation in the course of action. To act is to give oneself up. The Alcestis and Oedipus theme sublimated in *Electra* (Electra in relation to the deed treated with irony, it's true. Electra–Hamlet.)" Though an authentic clue to the place of *Electra* in Hofmannsthal's work, his comments do not account for the peculiarly hectic and hysterical mood of the play. A recent critic, Professor William H. Rey, has described *Electra,* the earlier *Alcestis,* and the later *Ödipus und die Sphinx* as "not tragedies in the strictest sense" but rather "mystery plays that rest on the dialectic of the tragic and the mystical." There is a valuable insight here into Hofmannsthal's serious plays generally, but the description still seems to fit *Jedermann, The Salzburg Great Theatre of the World,* and *The Tower* better than

Electra. One reason, perhaps, is that Hofmannsthal's notion of individuality and personality is itself ambiguous, since Electra's self-sacrifice or self-renunciation on one level is her self-fulfilment on another. Hofmannsthal indicated this ambiguity both in his reference to his ironic treatment of Electra's deed, and in another retrospective comment on the work: "All my three plays on ancient subjects are concerned with the dissolution of the concept of individuality. In *Electra* the individual is dissolved in the empirical way, inasmuch as the very substance of its life blasts it from within, as water about to freeze will crack an earthenware jug. Electra is no longer Electra, just because she has dedicated herself entirely to being Electra."

To say that *Electra* sacrifices herself, therefore, is not enough; she sacrifices one part of herself, her reason and common humanity, to another; and one cannot get away from the fact that this other part includes not only her super-ego but her subconscious compulsions. Hofmannsthal may have had this in mind when he wrote that Electra's individuality is "dissolved in the empirical way." Surely this serves to distinguish Electra's mode of self-sacrifice from that of the Beggar, say, in the late mystery play, or from Sigismund's in *The Tower.*

Other references to Electra in his notebooks and in *Ad me Ipsum* bear out Hofmannsthal's awareness of the distinction. Thus he mentions that when he first conceived the plan in September 1901, he wanted to write a work as different as possible from Goethe's *Iphigenia*, a work of which no one could say, as Goethe said of his *Iphigenia*, that "it was damnably humane" (*"verteufelt human"*). Between Goethe's "humane" and Hofmannsthal's "barbaric" treatment of Greek myths there lay not only Freud but Bachofen, Erwin Rohde, and Nietzsche, whose first major work had taken up Schopenhauer's critique of the "principle of individuation." When, in 1926, Hofmannsthal remarked that "Electra's deed springs from a kind of possession," he clearly indicated the pathological aspects of Electra's sacrifice; and in another passage of *Ad me Ipsum,* he explained in psychological terms Electra's difficulties in executing her deed, by observing that "action presupposes a transition from the conscious to the unconscious."

Nevertheless there is one related theme in *Electra* which undoubtedly links the play to the whole of Hofmannsthal's works, both early and late. The figure of Chrysothemis, Electra's sister, is contrasted with the heroine not only in her shrinking from the deed and her hope of fulfilment in marriage and motherhood but also in the desire to forget the past rather than lay its ghost by re-enacting it. No pre-occupation of Hofmannsthal's was more constant than the one to which these contrasted attitudes point; and it is Electra's heroic fixation on a single event, a single commitment, and a single continuity that relates her to the principal characters of Hofmannsthal's other comic and serious plays. The contrast and dialectic run through all his works, from the early verse plays to *Ariadne auf Naxos* and *The Difficult Man.* By a process common to many of Hofmannsthal's plays, the antinomy is subject to variations which sometimes seem to invert it. Whereas in the comedies marriage is presented as the state in which men and women establish the necessary continuity, and the adventurer or libertine stands for the opposite way, Electra's fixation on her murdered father assumes the kind of significance that marriage has in circumstances less extreme, and in fact makes the very idea of marriage impossible and loathsome to her. It is Chrysothemis who corresponds to the adventurers and libertines of the comedies in her failure to establish a higher continuity. To entertain human hopes in these particular circumstances, Electra suggests, is to be bestial. Here, as elsewhere, one can only commend Hofmannsthal's subordination of an ideal of abstract consistency to the psychological and imaginative demands of the specific case. Sigismund is another instance of a Hofmannsthal hero whose early circumstances place him both below and above common humanity and commit him to a kind of tie different from that between man and wife. It is not without significance that Electra and Chrysothemis have been reduced to a status scarcely less brutish than that of Sigismund in his tower. Of Orestes, too, we are told that "they gave him a wretched place to live" and that he was to have been killed in infancy, like Sigismund. The tower motif also appears in Hofmannsthal's next Greek play, *Ödipus und die Sphinx*. Oedipus says at one point:

> *Ich dachte, meinen Vater zu bitten um einen Turm,*
> *um ein Lager von Stroh und um schwere Ketten—*

(I wished to beg my father for a tower,
for a bed of straw and for heavy chains—)

And at another he speaks of a tower that "stands remote amid mountain chasms." Sigismund, after all, only just avoids parricide; and Oedipus, too, is obsessed by dreams that blur the "frontier between sleep and waking . . . between death and life." Like Electra, he has a horror of the sexual act as such, because he cannot dissociate it from an early trauma connected with his parents.

The precedent of *Hamlet*, to which Hofmannsthal alludes, may well be more relevant to the psychological motivation of his *Electra* and *Ödipus* plays than any discovery by Freud; and in any case the most characteristic thread in Hofmannsthal's *Electra* is the relation to time, and hence to personal identity, of the two sisters and of the mother. Clytemnestra, too, is self-estranged because she fails to connect the past with the present; but, unlike Chrysothemis, she doubts the very possibility of making the connection. If Electra resembles Hofmannsthal and his Lord Chandos in their "word-scepticism," Clytemnestra is equally sceptical of deeds. "Now it was before, and then it was past," she says of the murder of Agamemnon, and asks: "For am I still the same who has done the deed?" Here again she voices one of Hofmannsthal's first and last questions. Personal identity rests not on the cultivation of personality, but on loyalty to something that is not oneself. Electra has this kind of loyalty, Chrysothemis and Clytemnestra have not. Granted that this play is governed by a mystique less of the spirit than of the heart and blood, that it is set from beginning to end in a domain in which the bestial impinges on the human and superhuman, *Electra* is neither a freak nor an aberration in Hofmannsthal's work. Had Hofmannsthal succeeded in writing his projected Pentheus and Semiramis plays, to mention only two extraordinary works sketched out and abandoned at different periods of his life, *Electra* would hardly strike us as an isolated product of his imagination.

Electra's "word-scepticism" has been mentioned; but in Hofmannsthal's works "word-scepticism" always has its mystical corollary. "Hatred is nothing," she says,

> *er zehrt*
> *und zehrt sich selber auf, und Liebe ist*
> *noch weniger als Hass, sie greift nach allem*
> *und kann nichts fassen, ihre Hände sind*
> *wie Flammen, die nichts fassen, alles Denken*
> *ist nichts, und was aus einem Mund hervorkommt,*
> *ist ohnmächtige Luft, nur der ist selig,*
> *der seine Tat zu tuen kommt.*

(it eats and eats
and consumes itself, and love is still less
than hatred, it reaches after everything
and cannot grasp anything, its hands
are like flames which grasp nothing, all thinking
is nothing, and what issues from the mouth
is a powerless breeze, only he is blessed
who is coming to do his deed!)

Here the deed itself transcends its very object and motivation. The end in which Electra finds her fulfilment and liberation quite literally "dissolves her individuality." The dance in which she celebrates her fulfilment and liberation is not only "nameless," in the sense of indescribable or indefinable often given to it by Hofmannsthal, but beyond words *and* reason. It is the pure gesture to which both words and deeds can only approximate and aspire.

In the operatic version Hofmannsthal slightly elaborated the concluding dialogue. A duet between Electra and Chrysothemis is interpolated immediately before the dance. This is dominated by imagery of darkness and light, death and life. Electra sings:

> *Ich war ein Schwarzer Leichnam*
> *unter Lebenden, und diese Stunde*
> *bin ich das Feuer des Lebens und meine Flamme*
> *verbrennt die Finsternis der Welt.*
> *Mein Gesicht muss weisser sein*
> *als das weissglühende Gesicht des Monds.*
> *Wenn einer auf mich sieht,*
> *muss er den Tod empfangen oder muss*
> *vergehen vor Lust.*

> (I was a black corpse
> among the living and at this hour
> I am the fire of life, and my flame
> burns up the darkness of the world.

My face must be whiter
than the whitely glowing face of the moon.
If someone looks upon me
he must be struck dead
or be consumed with joy.)

To Chrysothemis' words "Now our brother is here and love flows over us like oil and myrrh, love is all! Who can live without love?" Electra replies:

Ai! Liebe tötet! aber keiner fährt dahin
und hat die Liebe nicht gekannt!

(Ai! Love kills! But no one passes on
and has not known love!)

This affirmation does not contradict Electra's earlier assertion that love is "nothing" or suggest any agreement between the two sisters. What is oil and myrrh to Chrysothemis is fuel to Electra's flame; her love can be neither thwarted nor gratified, because it has no object but to consume itself and her.

The free verse of *Electra* constitutes an important advance on the iambic blank verse of the *Alcestis* and of Hofmannsthal's own transitional verse plays. In one of these, *Der Abenteurer und die Sängerin*, he had used a mixture of regular iambic verse and prose. The free verse line of *Electra*, which he was to adopt for his libretti of the next twenty years, proved as suitable for lyrical climaxes as for trivial conversation. It was supple, often close to colloquial speech and speech rhythm, yet stylized without being stilted. It is no exaggeration to say that in regular blank verse Hofmannsthal's Electra would have been unbearable; the natural and easy way in which she can fall into the Austrian vernacular of Hofmannsthal's time distinguishes her from many other *fin de siècle* heroines, such as Wilde's *Salomé,* and saves

93

her from both preciousness and the neo-Shakespearean
rhetoric satirized by Max Beerbohm. The diction of *Electra*
is not obtrusively grand, exquisite, or memorable, but sub-
servient to the wordless gesture: it exactly fits the theme.
"In action, in deeds," Hofmannsthal said of the play, "the
enigmas of language are resolved."

IV

From *Electra* to *The Salzburg Great Theatre of the World—*
this leap in space, time, *ambiance,* and morality (both in the
sense of manners and of ethical absolutes) calls for some
agility on the reader's part. It may be as well to begin by
quoting Hofmannsthal's short preface to the play, written
for its publication as a book in 1922 and drawing on a note
appended to it when it appeared earlier that year in Hofmannsthal's periodical *Neue Deutsche Beiträge:*

> Everyone knows that there is a spiritual drama by Calderón
> called *The Great Theatre of the World.* From this play the whole
> pivotal metaphor has been borrowed: that the World erects a
> stage on which men enact the play of life in the roles allotted to
> them by God; also the title of this play and the names of the six
> characters who represent human life—and that is the whole ex-
> tent of the borrowing. Yet these constituents do not belong to the
> great Catholic poet as his invention, but are part of that treasury
> of myths and allegories which the Middle Ages shaped and be-
> queathed to later centuries.

Hofmannsthal refrains from justifying his adaptation
on dogmatic or ethical grounds. If an apology is implied in
the preface, it is an apology for the principle of adaptation itself, not for the particular work adapted or for its dogmatic
character; and Hofmannsthal did feel strongly about the
question of borrowings from other writers. Here again his atti-

tude involved a rejection of nineteenth-century individualism and of its highly developed sense of private property in the realms of art and ideas. In his *Book of Friends* Hofmannsthal included this definition of the writer from the preface to Lesage's *Gil Blas*: *"Un auteur est un homme qui trouve dans les livres tout ce qui lui trotte par la tête."* Had he wished to elaborate his defence against those who accused him of plagiarism, Hofmannsthal could have cited not only this older freedom to borrow and adapt, but the practice of many distinguished artists of his own time, including the most "modern" and original. As early as 1909 a hostile critic had written that Hofmannsthal was "fated to be a dilettante, a keeper of the museum of culture, as it were"; but this was before individualism had been shaken out of its smugness, and long before the more characteristically twentieth-century awareness of a *"musée imaginaire."*

Nevertheless, none of Hofmannsthal's works and activities more effectively antagonized the great majority of his former public and of the younger generation than his adaptations of *Everyman* and *El Gran Teatro del Mundo.* These plays were understood not as "myths" but as Christian tracts in dramatic form. Writing to Karl Kraus about the chances of having a play of her own put on, the poet Else Lasker-Schüler summed up the view common to most of the German *avant-garde* of the time: "Hofmannsthal of the tribe of teachers, I suppose, will object to it!" The same poet wrote a devastating account of Hofmannsthal's *Jedermann* in a letter to Herwarth Walden, editor of the Expressionist periodical *Die Aktion:*

For I've been to see Everyman or is it called All-Sorts? I think it is called All-Sorts for Everyman or Everyman for All-Sorts. Come in, ladies and gentlemen, to the giant Punch and Judy show. Where did it all come from? I think from the stables, Herwarth.

. . . Just think, if he'd taken to sculpture, if he'd taken to patching up sculpture, and fixed two new arms to the Venus de Milo! What literary things hasn't he dug up: first, the Oedipus of Sophocles, nourished with Viennese blood; and then he turned Electra into a demure schoolmistress! He lacks imagination. . . . The performance of *Jedermann* is an unartistic act, a shameful one.

However violent in its animus, Else Lasker-Schüler's indictment deserves to be taken seriously both because of her charge that Hofmannsthal lacked imagination—and she was by no means alone in making it—and because of her suggestion elsewhere in the letter that Hofmannsthal and Reinhardt were guilty of cynicism and hypocrisy in staging *Jedermann*: "Life and death, sin and judgment, Heaven and Hell—all are degraded to a spectacle, like those elephants and Arab horses decorated with ribbons and trinkets, yet not even for the delight of children as in that case, but for the edification of a rich sensation-hungry public." This criticism came from a fervently, though unconventionally, religious woman; and it raises questions that will continue to arise in the minds of readers and spectators of both plays.

In two essays on his *Jedermann*, published in 1911 and 1912, Hofmannsthal gave his own account of his reasons for writing this play; and most of what he says there applies equally to *The Salzburg Great Theatre of the World*. Hofmannsthal considers his dramatic adaptations generally, and remarks of *Jedermann*: "When I brought the play *Jedermann* on to the stage, I think it was not so much to add something to the German repertory as to restitute something that should have been part of it by rights, and of which it was deprived only by a kind of historical accident." This explains why Hofmannsthal abandoned an early attempt to write his play in prose and resorted to the irregular rhymed couplet made familiar to the German public by the sixteenth-century play-wright Hans Sachs (as well as by Goethe's *Faust*). To any contemporary who did not share Hofmannsthal's belief that "the powerful imagination is conservative," this kind of "restitution" was bound to smack of antiquarianism. Hofmannsthal's answer in the essay was: "In our time far too much fuss is made about our time"; and he justified his choice of the subject by calling it "a human fable in Christian dress."

"More and more," the second essay elaborates this description, "the true core revealed itself to me as humanly absolute, not part of any particular period, nor even inextricably bound up with Christian dogma. . . . For we are at bay and in the dark, in a different way from medieval man, but no less so: we have a wide perspective on many things, we can see through some things, and yet our true spiritual power of seeing is feeble; much is at our command, yet we are not commanders; what we should possess possesses us; and that which more than anything is a means, money, by a demonic inversion becomes our primary end."

Hofmannsthal also wrote a note on *The Salzburg Great Theatre of the World* for inclusion in a brochure on the Salzburg Festival (1925). By this time the theories of the Austrian literary historian Professor Josef Nadler, and of the poet and critic Rudolf Borchardt had begun to influence Hofmannsthal's thinking on cultural matters. The emphasis now falls less on the "humanly absolute" aspects of the fable, as on a particular South German and Austrian theatrical tradition which Nadler believed Hofmannsthal to represent in his time. To Borchardt Hofmannsthal owed some of his ideas about a "conservative revolution" that would do away with the evils of capitalism but preserve what was best in traditional values. These late preoccupations of Hofmannsthal, which made an increasing claim on him after Austria's defeat in the war, the partition of the Empire, and the Russian Revolution, were as controversial as any political commitment and open to misunderstandings that tend to arise wherever a primarily literary imagination impinges on political issues; but Hofmannsthal's sincerity is not in doubt. In all his works Hofmannsthal combined an extreme eclecticism in the choice of media with a constant and highly personal vision. What Else Lasker-Schüler regarded as a concession on Hofmannsthal's part to an amorphous "sensation-hungry" public sprang from his dominant need to merge his own individuality in impersonal conventions and to relate himself to the past. Else Lasker-Schüler's own works are individual in diction and form, and individualistic in attitude to the point of eccentricity; but her religious imagery reveals an eclecticism almost inescapable for any writer with a liberal bourgeois background, and more akin to Hofmannsthal's than she knew.

Hofmannsthal's interest in sociology, politics, and economics goes back to the beginning of the century and earlier, to his reading of works as diverse as *An Onlooker's Notebook* (articles from the *Manchester Guardian*) and Georg Simmel's *Philosophie des Geldes,* G. Lowes Dickinson's *A Modern Symposium* and the curious *Welt-Eroberung durch Heldenliebe* by Frederik van Eeden and Erich Gutkind. Hofmannsthal's annotations and marginalia in these books show that he envisaged a synthesis of socialist and conservative thinking—socialist in economics, conservative in all other regards. His political writings of the war years show much the same outlook, despite a growing concern with Austrian conditions, with Austria's past and Austria's future. It is in his writings and lectures in the post-war period that Hofmannsthal seemed to come closest to a political position well to the right of centre; but his cultural conservatism must not be confused with the economic conservatism of classes and groups. Just as Hofmannsthal added Mammon to the characters in *Jedermann* to give more scope to his own concern with modern acquisitiveness, so he invested the character of the Beggar in the later play with an importance derived from his own concern with the modern ideology of revolt. His inclusion of an Adversary and a Busybody serves to strengthen the same thread in the play.

If imagination is shown not in the invention of plots—and even the plot of Hofmannsthal's play is given an entirely new twist—but in the concealed presence everywhere "of the determining personality," Hofmannsthal's antiquarian re-creations are by no means unimaginative. Even his "word-scepticism" and "word-mysticism" make their appearance when World says: "He to whom fulness is given . . . his tongue is too heavy for speech." As for the Beggar's part in the play—both before and after his illumination—to dismiss it as "counter-revolutionary" or "reactionary," as critics continue to do, is to forget that Hofmannsthal was no ordinary conservative but the representative "of a society that does not exist."

In his lecture *The Poet in Our Time* (1906) Hofmannsthal had characterized the modern poet as living "Under the staircase, where all must pass him and no one pays any attention to him"; and in his copy of Simmel's *Philosophie des Geldes* Hofmannsthal had entered the words "the poet" against the Franciscan motto *"nihil habentes, omnia possedentes."* Hofmannsthal, therefore, was closely identified with the figure of the Beggar. His various writings and jottings on the problem of the modern "money nexus," to "get to the back of which," he noted, "may be the meaning of the moral and even religious revolution in which we seem to be involved," confirm that he added the weight of personal conviction to the Beggar's accusations in the play. When the Beggar says "that the world must be renewed," this, too, is Hofmannsthal's own conviction, and the renewal became the subject of his later play *The Tower*. That revolt is not enough, personal revenge and hatred—however justified— are not enough, is a moral that remains revolutionary even in our time.

Other interrelations in the play that had a special significance for Hofmannsthal are those between Beauty and the King and between Beauty, the Beggar, and Wisdom. Beauty, in the play, condemns the Beggar for his physical ugliness; and it is only towards the end of the play that the King realizes the difference between "seeming and being," paying tribute to Wisdom's power to fuse both into a "higher light." This is the neo-Platonism that helped Hofmannsthal himself to overcome the "introverted" mysticism of his youth and the autonomous aestheticism which his early works were once thought to exemplify.

V

The Tower, too, began as the free adaptation of a play by Calderón which Hofmannsthal undertook in 1902. Though even this early version anticipated some of the drastic changes which make Hofmannsthal's post-war play an entirely original work, he took over the trochaic verse from Calderón's play *Life Is a Dream,* and this proved a most unsatisfactory medium. At this time Hofmannsthal was drawn to the subject mainly because of its symbolic parallels with his own "pre-existence"; what attracted him, he wrote in a letter of 1904, was "to descend into the ultimate depths of the dubious cave kingdom 'I' and discover the no-longer-I or the world." This theme remained prominent in the later play, but the "world" presented in it had become incomparably more various and complex than that of the Spanish play or of Hofmannsthal's early adaptation. Even in this early adaptation Hofmannsthal had tried to work out a new interrelation of the subsidiary characters both with one another and with Sigismund, but the "almost insuperable difficulties" had defeated him.

Hofmannsthal returned to the subject in 1918, and completed one version of *The Tower* in 1925. The "almost insuperable difficulties" remained, and, as Hofmannsthal wrote in 1910 about his trochaic adaptation, these difficulties were not so much of an artistic as of an intellectual kind. If Hofmannsthal was never quite satisfied with the 1925 version of *The Tower*—and his complete re-working of the play in 1927 suggests that he was not satisfied—one reason is that it was more to him than a play; amongst other things it was his reckoning with the post-war world, a last attempt to embody the substance of his own life in a myth, and a kind of moral and spiritual testament.

The 1925 version of *The Tower* presents two main difficulties. One has to do with the interrelation of the main characters and of the political or ideological powers which they represent. The other has to do with the ultimate implications of Sigismund's life and death. Hofmannsthal himself found it difficult to comment on the significance of the different characters and factions.

The poet's starting-point is the figures themselves; they appear to him, but at the same time they appear to him as a configuration of destinies. Their destiny consists in existing together (the mystery of contemporaneousness). But by crossing one another's paths, they influence one another, not in a particular way, not dialectically, not even by their characters, as in Shakespeare, but by their total volume, like stars. They hardly speak to one another, but each really only speaks to himself. By turns they mean something to one another that exceeds human standards: thus to his father Sigismund means revolt, revolution; and to Sigismund the latter means all that demands reverence but also all that is oppressive, all that is frightening. . . . Thus beside the legitimate King there appear his spiritual adviser and, at the same time, the worldly, political side of the Church. Opposed to them, Olivier, the revolt of the underdog, the perennially ochlocratic element. Julian is the most difficult to define: he is worldly wisdom, the gifted individual's craving for power, but he is denied the grace of *kairos*—his endeavours are in vain, are frustrated—and yet again they are not: he too has a part in Sigismund's destiny. The Children's King, to me, is like a reborn Sigismund: hence the brotherly note between them, their rapid, wholly reciprocal understanding.

It is characteristic of Hofmannsthal that several of the subsidiary figures in the play combine traits borrowed from many disparate literary or historical persons. The important character of the Doctor, for instance—important because exemplary in his unselfish devotion to Sigismund, his wisdom, and his penetration—draws on Paracelsus and the alchemical tradition ("There are connections everywhere"), Kierkegaard ("a strong will . . . a strong faith: the two are one"), and on the modern psychologists and physicians who have based their practice on the assumption that body and psyche are interdependent. The Grand Almoner of the play recalls Dostoevski's Grand Inquisitor ("an old man, almost ninety, tall and erect, with a withered face and sunken eyes"), but also certain features of Father Zossima in the same novel and of historical ecclesiastics of the seventeenth century. Hofmannsthal's primary source for the character of Olivier was Grimmelshausen's novel of the Thirty Years' War, *Der abenteuerliche Simplicissimus*, in which there is a marauder and thief of that name; but the affinities of Hofmannsthal's Olivier

extend from sixteenth- and seventeenth-century rebels to recent revolutionary leaders of the extreme Left and the extreme Right.

The most purely mythical figures in *The Tower* are the
Children's King and the Gipsy. Neither appears in the later
version of the play, which simplifies and clarifies the action in
many respects. The relative merits of the two versions remain controversial, and they cannot be discussed in detail
here; in a sense the two versions should be regarded as two
distinct works, the first more dreamlike, mythical, and utopian, the second more outward-looking, more clear-cut, and
more starkly tragic in its conclusion. That Hofmannsthal
should have written these two very different versions of the
play sheds some light on the struggles and uncertainties of his
last years, his premonitions of upheavals even greater than
those of the First World War, and his doubts as to the outcome. The Children's King is the embodiment of Hofmannsthal's hope that the new order would be ruled not by the
Oliviers of this world, but by Sigismund's spiritual successors.
Sigismund himself has to die in both versions for reasons to
which the figure of the Gipsy offers one clue; but in the later
version he is shot by Olivier's men, and Olivier himself remains triumphant at the end, having gained the upper hand
over Julian, over the conservative nobility, and over Sigismund's followers among the commoners and the poor.

The political configuration is necessarily complex in both
versions; it is its complexity that makes it both lifelike and
widely relevant. Motives everywhere are mixed, and Hofmannsthal does not reduce them to a neat pattern in black and
white. In the late version even Olivier appears less black,
partly because his bragging in the first scene is omitted, and
it is the other soldiers who praise his formidable qualities.
Julian's role becomes no less ambiguous in itself, but his part

in the revolution is hinted at already in the first act when he is seen giving a secret order to Olivier. The later acts show clearly that Julian has tried to control all the various factions, including the dissident nobles and high functionaries as well as Olivier's mob, mainly by playing off one against the other. At his instigation, members of Basilius' own Court and Cabinet force the King to abdicate in Sigismund's favour, only to be dismissed in turn by Julian. Basilius himself is banished to the Tower. It is Sigismund's refusal to play his part in Julian's machinations that leaves a power vacuum ultimately filled by Olivier. All these complicated issues are presented more briefly and succinctly in the 1927 version; and even the outward motivation of the central tragedy, Sigismund's, is more clearly defined. Yet some of the more mysterious motifs that go back to Hofmannsthal's first concern with the subject are lost in this tidying up. The episode of the Gipsy and her part in Sigismund's death are a case in point. Hofmannsthal's many drafts and notes for the play show that at one time Sigismund was to die of the plague as soon as he settled in one place; and elsewhere Hofmannsthal interpreted the Gipsy's role as the "vengeance of the material, maternal, time-bound." Though never made explicit anywhere in the play, this motif can still be "intuited" in the 1925 version, but it has no place in the more condensed and outwardly plausible plot of the 1927 version. This motif links up with Sigismund's asceticism everywhere in the play, with his remark, "But we have nothing else that could be our mother but this sex, and this is the substance of which the world is made," and with the Gipsy's pregnancy, to which the remark alludes. In this connection it is of some interest that Hofmannsthal read Claudel while drafting *The Tower,* and marked certain passages in *La Ville* that develop a religious and mystical symbolism of motherhood. Sigismund's remark may well be an

adaptation of one such passage, marked by Hofmannsthal in
1919: *"A qui, dans l'étreinte sacrée, restituerons-nous qu'à
l'épouse/La vie que nous devons à la mère."*

The implication could be that Sigismund's estrangement
from the feminine element, identified in his remark and in
Hofmannsthal's draft with matter (*materia*) itself, makes him
incomplete and vulnerable. The earlier scene with the Peasant Woman, his foster mother, and Julian's claim that he was
father and mother to Sigismund, support the implication, as
does Sigismund's obsession with the sow that eats her new-
born litter. If we remember Hofmannsthal's early preoccupation with Bachofen's "mother-right" and with the advantages
of matriarchy—best exemplified in his special cult of the Empress Maria Theresia—as well as his wholly unpuritanical
orientation in other works, the motif becomes far from insig-
nificant. Indeed it becomes a key to Sigismund's personal, as
distinct from political, tragedy.

It is nowhere suggested that Sigismund has incurred guilt
in forsaking his "pre-existence" in the tower and assuming the
active functions of ruler and military commander. These
functions are thrust upon him, and he remains true to his past.
Yet there is a certain inconsistency between his messianic
aspirations and his resort, in the last act, to such traditional
measures as the threatened hanging of twelve of his own
Tartars as a warning to other incendiaries. This inconsistency
between Sigismund's dreams and "the language of the world"
points to the primary tragic factor which dominates the 1927
version, and which Hofmannsthal could only mitigate in the
earlier version by the arrival of the utopian figure of the Children's King. The Children's King, however, and his community also differ from Sigismund in their happier relationship
to nature and the material world. This brings us back once
more to a deficiency in Sigismund, for which he is not to

blame—a guilt like that in certain Greek tragedies, like original sin, or like the complexes and traumas of modern psychology in that it does not arise from a specific or deliberate
transgression. That Hofmannsthal was no abstract moralist
can also be seen in his treatment of Sigismund's physical attack on Basilius; this is justified not ethically but psychologically, and it follows inevitably from what we know of Sigismund's early confinement in the Tower and his battles with
animals and vermin. Basilius, too, is an ambiguous figure. He
seems only too well related to nature and to *materia* in every
sense, but rather in the manner of Hofmannsthal's adventurer
figures who are slaves to the moment. His Christian devotions
are more conventional than real; that is why he is excessively
dependent on his spiritual and worldly advisers. He resembles
Julian, his political opponent, in being essentially vain and
hollow; the Doctor's diagnosis of Julian's sickness and the
Grand Almoner's of the King's are mutually complementary.
Body and soul, Hofmannsthal insists everywhere, must be at
one. In this way the characters of Julian and Basilius cast an
oblique light on Sigismund's (and vice versa), but especially
on Sigismund's ultimate failure to do justice to the material
world and to time. The phantasmagoric episode with the
Gipsy Woman serves to show that though familiarity has
made Sigismund proof against the cruder mysteries of the
"black" and bestial domains, his balance lacks this necessary,
merely human, centre. His mission, therefore, is only partly
fulfilled; he is an exemplary, but transitional, figure, and
the new order has still to be established by his successors.

The distinction of *The Tower,* both in absolute sense and
in the context of Hofmannsthal's work as a whole, need
hardly be stressed again here. It is the one completed work of
Hofmannsthal that fully engaged all his disparate faculties
and energies—the mystical and the worldly, the visionary and

the analytical, the adventurous and the conservative—and co-ordinated his many-sided experience within a single imaginative structure. Sigismund's emergence from the dream of pre-existence into a world torn apart by conflicting ambitions, interests, and vanities corresponded to the course of Hofmannsthal's own life; and Hofmannsthal was left with the knowledge that no existing society had any real use for what he had tried to give it. Yet he had been "here," and had done what he could.

Dramatically the earlier and richer version of *The Tower* almost exceeds the capacities of the stage as well as the capacities of most audiences. Yet in recent years it is the earlier version that has tempted producers, despite the technical difficulties. Though the play may never become popular or frequent on the stage, "the fascination of what's difficult" should save it from being finally banished to the printed page. In diction it is an effective and unique amalgam of poetic and vernacular, seventeenth-century and modern elements. A present-day reader may be struck by occasional similarities with the diction of Brecht, especially in his *Mother Courage*, which also draws on the characters and idiom of Grimmelshausen's novel; and the two dramatists have a great deal in common, not least the tendency to appropriate, fuse, and remould the most diverse material. Both were accused of plagiarism in their time; and both, for rather different reasons, were indifferent to the laws of private property in literature. Both needed to lose themselves in order to find themselves.

VI

Hofmannsthal's comedies represent the social side of his nature, his Austrian, as distinct from German, characteristics, his strongly developed historical sense, and his interest in manners both as a means of communication between individuals and as an indispensable defence of their ultimate privacy. Just as there are comic ingredients in *The Salzburg Great Theatre of the World* and in *The Tower*—the characters of the Peasant and of Anton are instances; and Calderón, like Shakespeare, provided a precedent for the mixture—there are tragic or mystical strands in the comedies. Easily though Hofmannsthal seemed to move in the social element, there were moments when it became transparent, when the necessary artifice of manners became an empty container and even his comic characters must face the abyss. Indeed, his great temptation as a writer of comedies was to conceal too much depth on the surface, too many intricate connections and metaphysical undertones. Like his magnificent fragment of a novel *Andreas,* the early comedy *Silvia im "Stern"* came to grief for that reason; and even *Cristinas Heimreise,* a work of the same period, only just supports the weight of its symbolism.

Here the discipline of collaboration proved a distinct advantage. The final version of *The Cavalier of the Rose* owes much of its success to the limitations of opera, to Strauss's insistence on a simple and conventionally comic plot, and his inability to cope with Hofmannsthal's psychological or metaphysical subtleties. Remarkably enough, this discipline and Hofmannsthal's drastic concessions to Strauss scarcely detracted from the literary merits of the libretto. The discarded second act, which has now been published in its original form, is dispensable to any reader of the play not principally concerned with Hofmannsthal's ideas or with his progress as a writer of comedies. Though Hofmannsthal wrote to Strauss that the finished work did not *wholly* satisfy him "as a fusion of word and music," the play as such is in no way inferior to his other comedies of this decade. Hofmannsthal could afford to sacrifice quite a number of his peculiar subtleties and profundities without becoming trite or superficial.

Hofmannsthal himself wrote in 1927 that this "libretto was the most untranslatable in the world" because its diction is no mere pastiche of eighteenth-century Viennese but "the imaginary language of the time." This applies to all Hofmannsthal's comedies (and to *The Tower*, whose diction and setting are those of an *imaginary* seventeenth century). The nineteenth-century setting of *Arabella* provided Hofmannsthal with yet another kind of linguistic raw material; since its imaginative restyling was less thorough than in other works, a neutral equivalent for its Viennese forms was more easily available. It is *The Difficult Man* that most stubbornly defies translation, for Hofmannsthal's highly stylized recasting of an aristocratic idiom—itself with no counterpart in the usage of any twentieth-century English social set—had to be reproduced in a colloquial prose that could take no subterfuge in poetic licence. Yet the delicate balance between artifice and realism would have been utterly upset if the translator had resorted to a style reminiscent of Sheridan or the Restoration dramatists, who did command an idiom at once precious and earthy enough to correspond to the hyper-Viennese, hyper-aristocratic style in this play.

The diction of *The Cavalier of the Rose* is more highly wrought than that of *Arabella*, less so than that of *The Difficult Man*. As in *Electra*, Hofmannsthal was able to combine natural speech rhythm with a poetic tautening and condensing of language. In exactly the same way, the historical and social milieu is treated naturalistically, yet with a concealed layer of mythical and utopian allusion. One instance is the very simple yet magical identification of the Princess with the Empress whose name she bears, and in whose reign the action falls. By the simple device of calling the Princess Marie

Thérèse, Hofmannsthal associates her not only with his favourite Austrian monarch but with those matriarchal virtues which the Empress exemplified in his eyes. What these virtues were can be seen in Hofmannsthal's essay on Maria Theresia, published in 1917, and more clearly still in a series of jottings in his copy of La Bruyère's *Les Caractères* (probably the nucleus of his essay). Here Hofmannsthal notes Maria Theresia's naïveté and her strength—which he calls "mother-strength"—her characteristically Austrian outlook and her capacity to "educate by example"; the most significant remark of all points to Bachofen's characterization of matriarchal societies: "Men, among the Germans, lacking in instinct. Service has to take the place of honour. Marlborough." (Marlborough, it seems likely, is cited as an example of a man not lacking in instinct.)

There is no reason, of course, why any listener or reader should be aware of the precise associations I have traced here; but any reader or listener who is at all attentive to the whole work, and to the Princess's role in it, will sense the degree to which this figure dominates the action, educating by example, shaming Ochs not by snubbing him but by opposing her finer instincts to his crude and dishonourable conduct, and giving her blessing at the end to the union of two classes. On the surface *The Cavalier of the Rose* is a conventional comedy with farcical elements; but the infiltration of a concealed myth also turns it into a social allegory at once historical and utopian (because exemplary). Here the depths have been successfully concealed in the surface.

By the same imaginative fusion, the love affair between the Princess and Octavian has been cryptically mythologized; and it is a tribute to Hofmannsthal's tact to repeat that no one need be conscious of the submerged myth. It matters little whether we accept the opening love scene because it fits in with our ideas of eighteenth-century morals, because it is true to the emotional needs of this particular woman, evidently childless and close to middle age, or because it is part of the political and social allegory and tallies with the concealed myth of the matriarch. All these layers are inseparable. The grave undertones—Hofmannsthal's own recurrent question "What does the you mean, what you and I," and the related question of personal identity in time—help to define the peculiar tenderness of a love always on the verge of renunciation. "Easy is what we must be—holding and taking, holding and letting go"—this not only takes us back to the roots of Hofmannsthal's work, to the early poems and verse plays, but sums up the whole libretto, its lightness and its profundity; for these words apply not only to the Princess's love for Octavian and his for her, but to the allegory and to the myth. Hofmannsthal's ideal ruler knows that tradition embraces flux and change, that the old order must be made to merge gently in the new if continuity is to be maintained. (In the same way Sigismund in *The Tower* tells the Bannerets at the end that the old nobility will have to renounce their powers and privileges under the new dispensation.) The woman and lover of the first scene is in no way inconsistent with the Princess and matriarchal figure of the last: the quality of Marie Thérèse's love for Octavian prepares us for the delicacy and generosity of mind required for her final renunciation, her social mediation and the reminder to Ochs that his game, too, is up.

For his essay on Maria Theresia, Hofmannsthal chose an epigraph from the historian Adam Müller: "The State is an alliance of past generations with later ones, and vice versa." The relevance of this motto extends to Hofmannsthal's political attitude generally, to the role of the Princess in this libretto, and to an awareness of the past not only in society, but in each individual's life, that distinguished Hofmannsthal and his characters. In her love for Octavian the Princess tries to link her own past with the present and the future, yet knows all the time that another will have to take her place. Sophie and Octavian, too, have a part in this counterpoint of past and present. Though they fall in love at first sight, their love has a prehistory, a pre-existence, as every truly decisive moment has in Hofmannsthal. Octavian tries to express this sense of prehistory in a reminiscence of his childhood. Sophie, more concretely, has prepared herself for the encounter by a girlishly snobbish study of Octavian's pedigree.

In all his comedies, if not in all his dramatic works, Hofmannsthal was more concerned with the relation between individuals—the "space between characters that is mystically alive" of his Shakespeare lecture, a space that could be filled by the dead or by something other than the persons in question—than with the individual's psychology. In his 1927 postscript to *The Cavalier of the Rose* he wrote that "Molière's comedies, too, rest not so much on the characters themselves as on the relations of the often very typical figures to one another." Nevertheless, in the discarded second act Hofmannsthal had done more to bring out Sophie's growth into an individual. At one point there Octavian says to her:

> *Erst muss Sie selber sich helfen!*
> *Dann hilf ich Ihr auch!*
> *Tu Sie das erste für mich,*
> *dann tu ich was für Sie.*

> (First you must help yourself
> then I will help you too.
> You do the first thing for me
> then I'll do something for you.)

This, perhaps, would have sounded too deliberately moralizing a note, and the Octavian of the final version is more gallant in his readiness to take Sophie as she is; but in the words of a perceptive critic, Franz Tumler, the lines serve to show that "members of the new society now being shaped must fulfil this harder demand to justify themselves as persons; they are entering an order whose values have ceased to be aristocratic." The old aristocratic order, the same critic says, placed all the stress not on the individual's character but on his rank: and it is true that Ochs's behaviour is justified in his own eyes by his rank alone, as he repeatedly makes clear. Because the Princess understands both codes, she can mediate between them in the last scene. Even then she does not appeal to Ochs's honour as an individual—far less to any puritanical code which no character in the play observes—but reminds him that this is his last chance to save his face as a man of the world. At the same time we know that a whole social class is being asked to retire decently; like the paralysed old nobleman with the symbolic name Greifenklau ("griffin's claw"), it has come to the end of its predatory reign. Yet an alliance of the old with the new has been effected.

A similar social allegory is contained in *Arabella,* though the texture of this work is thinner and less rich. The nobility, by now, has been well and truly displaced. Count Waldner and his family live in an hotel (based on the Ungarische Krone, an hotel near St. Stephen's Cathedral, Vienna, frequented by the country gentry on their visits to the capital even in Hofmannsthal's time) and can no more afford two marriageable daughters than their temporary quarters. Hofmannsthal's main difficulty here was that by the time he wrote the libretto even this historical phase was a thing of the past; his hope, before and during the war, that the Empire might be saved by a fuller integration of the non-German nationalities had been defeated by their secession. In *The Cavalier of the Rose,* Croatia is a remote region where the Marshal hunts bear and lynx; in *Arabella* it comes to Vienna in the person of Mandryka to save the fortunes of the Waldner family; but by 1927 it was part of a foreign nation, Yugoslavia, and the Waldners of the time were either coming to terms with the little Austrian Republic and their reduced status in it, or placing their hopes in its union with a larger, more prosperous, and more industrialized Germany. These realities cast their shadow on *Arabella;* though Hofmannsthal agreed with Novalis that after a lost war one should write comedies, *Arabella* lacks the mythical undertones of the pre-war work. Hofmannsthal's social utopia, by this time, lay at the far end of tragic processes; and all the waltzes of Vienna could not drown the rumble of that apocalypse which had been his theme in *The Tower.*

"The Prussian threatens to the left, the Russian to the right," Adelaide elaborates on Dominic's truly Austrian remark that "we are always poised on the edge of an abyss." Champagne, waltzes, and love, if not guardian angels, were still an effective remedy in 1860, but Hofmannsthal could not lend much conviction to them in 1928; and when Adelaide exclaims "O Vienna! City of scandal and intrigue!" a real and recurrent complaint of his own was also voiced by Hofmannsthal. Ochs's version of it in the earlier libretto is that of a country gentleman confronted with an alien code, and caught in the snares of newfangled institutions; in *Arabella* it is not Mandryka, the true stranger to Vienna, who makes it, but the more sophisticated Adelaide.

The symbolism of the glass of water (and its association with the healthy, primitive order represented by Mandryka and his forests) almost provides a substitute for the myth; but it is more deliberate, less organic, than the concealed depths of *The Cavalier of the Rose,* just as the contrast between the characters of the two sisters is less subtly drawn than in Hofmannsthal's earlier treatment of the subject in his story *Lucidor.* Yet *Arabella* has other virtues, apart from its merit as a libretto. Together with *The Cavalier of the Rose* and *The Difficult Man* it can be read as part of a trilogy embodying Austrian manners and Austrian history—always with the proviso that Hofmannsthal's true domain was not the realism but the symbolism of manners. Waldner's gambling, Adelaide's selling of her jewellery and her trust in the fortune-teller, Mandryka's wad of bank notes—the proceeds of his sale of *real* estate—all such details are at once realistic and at least as telling as the obvious symbolism of the glass of water.

As in other works, Hofmannsthal also conveys his distinctly Austrian and unpuritanical morality, though the prominence given to Arabella almost blurs Zdenka's more truly heroic role. Arabella, of course, is more dignified and more conventionally admirable; but it is relatively easy to be dignified when one knows that both the truth and convention are on one's side. Hofmannsthal's true heroines, like Helen in *The Difficult Man* and Zdenka in *Arabella,* take greater risks and know that social conventions may have to be broken for love's sake. As Arabella herself admits, it is Zdenka who has "the kinder heart" and has taught her

> *dass wir nichts wollen dürfen, nichts verlangen,*
> *abwägen nicht und markten nicht und geizen nicht,*
> *nur geben und liebhaben immerfort!*

> (that we should not want anything, nor ask for anything,
> not calculate and not barter and not covet,
> only give and go on loving always.)

In her lack of calculation Zdenka resembles not only Helen, but the most completely realized of all Hofmannsthal's comic figures, The Difficult Man himself.

If *The Tower* is the most daring of Hofmannsthal's non-operatic plays, *The Difficult Man* is the most nearly perfect. Beneath its unbroken surface it holds greater tensions, cross-currents, and whirlpools than any comparable work in the classical repertory. Indeed its classicism is deceptive; once again Hofmannsthal had set himself the task of creating a classical convention in a modern void. Much as the play owes to Molière, Goldoni, Marivaux, Sheridan, Lessing, and all those comic masterpieces which Hofmannsthal had assiduously studied and emulated, *The Difficult Man* has no precedent in Austrian literature and only a superficial affinity with foreign models. Even Molière in his *Misanthrope*, whose hero seems to foreshadow the individualism of a later age, did not span such distances. Hofmannsthal's Difficult Man is at once the representative of a society that Hofmannsthal had to invent for the purpose of his play, and a man beyond society for reasons that Hofmannsthal indicated in a letter about his play to Anton Wildgans in 1921:

You will find that in it I have hidden all that sprang from my own soul, all that was personally metaphysical, or as you like to call it, "confessional," under the irony of its figuration—as in *Cristina,* but in this case even under the double irony of its figuration in the social, preconditioned element. And yet this individual, metaphysical *core* is very strong, and I was afraid at times that it would break the shell.

It is the problem that has often tormented and oppressed me (already in *Death and the Fool*), most acutely in the *Letter of Lord Chandos,* which perhaps you know: How does the lonely individual come to commit himself to society through language, indeed, how does he come to be connected to it through language whether he likes it or not, inextricably? And also: how can the speaking man act, when to speak is to understand, and to understand is to be incapable of action—my personal, never-ceasing concern with the perennial antinomy between speaking and doing, knowing and living. . . .

The distance spanned by Hofmannsthal in this comedy is that between a society itself ideal because it has the consistency and style of a work of art, and a character who has experienced that almost mystical detachment from all human institutions, that extreme isolation, which Hofmannsthal knew to be a peculiarity of his own time. To span such a distance in a comedy that never ceases to be social called for consummate art. Even historically, the social world of *The Difficult Man* lies at one remove from any reality that an audience of 1921 might have taken to be their own. The time of the action is not specified, but Hofmannsthal wrote the play during the war and appears to have planned it as early as 1908. The actual conditions of the immediate post-war period, the defeat and dissolution of the Austrian Empire, the social revolution and economic straits, do not impinge on the setting. One thinks of Proust's world rather than that of any distinctly post-war writer, or, closer to Hofmannsthal in more than locality, of Robert Musil's retrospective novel *The Man without Qualities*. Yet neither recollection nor caricature accounts for the special *ambiance* of Hofmannsthal's twentieth-century aristocracy, and the reason is that Hofmannsthal had created this world as the representative of a society that did not exist, incorporating so many historical and national traits that no one need suspect him of creating an utopia.

One possible analogy is the Ireland of Synge and Synge's deceptive use of a diction which the uninitiated would call naturalistic, though in the later plays it is as much a distillation and stylization of colloquial usage as the language of Hofmannsthal's aristocrats. The precise character of Hofmannsthal's Austrian utopia—as distinct from the Germany represented in the play by Neuhoff—is defined in Hofmannsthal's table entitled "Prussian and Austrian," of 1917, drawn up when he had begun to have second thoughts about the military alliance and its consequences:

As a whole

PRUSSIA	AUSTRIA
Created, an artificial structure, a country poor by nature,	Grown, historical tissue, a country rich by nature,
all in men and by men,	all from the outside: from nature and God,
hence: held together by a belief in the State,	held together by a love of home,
more virtue,	more piety,
more efficiency	more humanity

Social Structure

PRUSSIA	AUSTRIA
A loose social texture, the classes divided by cultural differences; but a precise machinery	A dense social texture, the classes unified by culture; the mechanics of the whole imprecise
The lesser nobility sharply distinct, consistent in itself	High nobility rich in types, politically inconsistent
Homogeneous officialdom: embodying *one* spirit. "Dominant" attitudes and customs	Heterogeneous officialdom: no prescribed way of thinking or feeling
The people: the most easily disciplined mass, unlimited authority (army; scientific social democracy)	The people: most independent mass, unlimited individualism
Supreme authority of the Crown	Supreme confidence in the Crown

The Individual

THE PRUSSIAN	THE AUSTRIAN
Up to date in his views (cosmopolitan around 1800, liberal around 1848, now Bismarckian, almost without a memory for past phases)	Traditional in his views, stable almost for centuries
Lacks a sense of history	Possesses an instinct for history
Strength of abstractions	Little talent for abstractions
Incomparable in orderly execution	More quick on the uptake
Acts according to instructions	Acts according to fitness
Strength of dialectic	Rejection of dialectic
More skill in expression	More balance
More consequential	More ability to adapt himself to conditions
Self-reliance	Self-irony
Seemingly masculine	Seemingly immature
Makes everything functional	Gives a social twist to everything
Asserts and justifies himself	Prefers to keep things vague
Self-righteous, arrogant, hectoring	Shamefaced, vain, witty
Forces crises	Avoids crises
Fights for his rights	Lets things go
Incapable of entering into other people's thoughts	Enters into other people's thoughts to the point of losing his character
Willed character	Play-acting
Every individual bears a part of authority	Every individual bears a part of all humanity
Pushing	Pleasure-seeking
Preponderance of the occupational	Preponderance of the private
Extreme exaggeration	Irony to the point of self-destruction

What is most striking about the scheme is that Austria has those instinctive and organic qualities which Bachofen had attributed to the matriarchal order, whereas Prussia is all "masculine" artifice and will. In drawing up the scheme and in his confrontation of Hans Karl and Helen with Theophilus Neuhoff, Hofmannsthal was aware of his own relations to men like Stefan George, who had once admonished Hofmannsthal for refusing to become his partner in a joint dictatorship over German literature. (To be more precise, Hofmannsthal had not refused, but had evaded the issue and gone his own way—in typically Austrian fashion.) At one time the play was to be called *The Man without Designs;* and the whole society which Hans Karl at once represents and avoids is characterized by its disapproval of anything that is too deliberate. Crescence has designs of a practical and maternal kind; but when these are thwarted by events, she is quite happy to let them go. Even Stani, a member of the younger generation who believes in steering a definite course, accepts the unpredictable with good grace. Clearly a nation or a class or an individual so purely Austrian in this regard could not survive for long; and both the play and the table show a sharp awareness of this danger. In the play the awareness takes the form of irony: faced with a man without designs, Helen, in the end, is forced to break her own code by reversing the conventional roles and proposing marriage to a man. To be wholly without designs is to be "like a child," as Helen says of Hans Karl, and to run the risk of self-destruction in a competitive world.

The Austrians, according to Hofmannsthal's table, reject every abstract dialectic. Although a great deal of theory is concealed in the play—Hofmannsthal's borrowings from Kierkegaard are one instance—a delicate interplay of characters and ironies takes the place of a deliberate dialectic, thesis, or moral. The implications of this interplay are almost inexhaustible because the work remains "open" in a way which almost suggests that its author, too, was a man without designs. Needless to say, this very openness was the product of Hofmannsthal's intricate art. There is scarcely a sentence in *The Difficult Man* that does not reveal some new aspect of a character or of a relationship between characters, adding to the significance of the whole. To disentangle this web and comment on the function of each thread in turn would require an essay at least as long as Professor Emil Staiger's brilliant and satisfying study of the play. Since this study is itself a highly organized work of art, no extract from it would amount to an interpretation of the play as a whole, and I shall attempt no such interpretation of my own. A few hints will have to suffice here.

Once again a symbolism of names points to some of the more obvious connections and antinomies. Two characters not quite at home in the social world of the play incorporate the particle *Neu* (new) in their names: Neuhoff, the German aristocrat, and Neugebauer, the secretary whose disapproval of his employer's sheltered life is intimated at one point. Both names also suggest a formerly rural order, as opposed to the combination of "old" with "town" in the surname of Helen and her father. Helen's Christian name needs no comment, but Hans Karl's surname may well indicate his role of lover (*buhlen*, to love; *Buhle*, lover)—which he performs so incompetently—and offer a clue to his inmost nature, a capacity for love, tenderness, and sympathy so great that it becomes a danger to him and to others, especially in conjunction with his extreme aversion to declarations, explanations, and confessions. How much of himself Hofmannsthal put into this bizarre and complicated character must be apparent to any perceptive reader.

The name Vincent explains itself; a double irony—Vincent fails to conquer—connects the servant both with Neuhoff, the designing, deliberate, and self-assured German suitor who at once admires and despises the world into which he has intruded, and with a new social order impatient to displace the "degenerate" aristocracy of the play. His antipoles are Lukas and Agathe, whose names evoke Christian associations and an old master-servant relationship deeply rooted in the Austrian tradition. This Austrian tradition, in turn, derived from the Spanish. The roles of Anton in *The Tower* and of his prototype Clarin in Calderón's *Life Is a Dream* are more relevant to it than those of the servants in Molière's comedies. In Hofmannsthal, as in Spanish plays, a religious and mystical significance attaches to the relationship and to the notion of service generally, and the prominence of the relationship in works by Cervantes, Calderón, and Tirso de Molina was carried over into Austrian plays by Grillparzer, Raimund, and Nestroy. Hofmannsthal's later comedy *Der Unbestechliche* (1923) hinges on the relationship: here it is the incorruptible, but far from impeccable, servant Theodore —a symbolic name once more—who dominates the action and prevents his master from betraying the old values.

Antoinette's affinities, on the other hand, are French, eighteenth-century, rococo; but they extend to the Venetian figures of Hofmannsthal's early comedies and of his novel *Andreas*, to Zerbinetta in his *Ariadne auf Naxos*, and to all those of his characters who agree with Antoinette that "all beginnings are beautiful" and "the only thing that's real to me is what I have at any one moment." Yet by one of those reversals that prove Hofmannsthal an ironist rather than a dialectician, she can turn the tables on Hans Karl and present him as the faithless and fickle seducer; for though her memory is short on the whole, in this one instance she did commit herself—to the one man who, apart from her husband, had no designs on her. Hans Karl, it seems, had always wanted to lead her back to the only commitment that is valid in his eyes, her first and last commitment to her husband; but in doing so he comes up against the consequences of having no designs and no confidence in speech, "that indecent excess of self-esteem." Only religious love can presume to be impersonal; by practising altruism on Antoinette, Hans Karl has gone too far and precipitated something more serious, for once, than a mere muddle or misunderstanding. As for the outcome, Hofmannsthal wisely left the ends loose; but Antoinette's treatment of Neuhoff and her encounter with her transmogrified husband suggest that all may yet be well.

For all his seeming roughness, Hechingen himself has many facets. To Hans Karl he stands for a partly inarticulate decency, loyalty, and lovingness, a humility and self-effacement comparable to that of the clown Furlani. Hans Karl's nephew sees only the clownishness of Hechingen, since Stani lacks Hans Karl's mystical unworldliness. Furlani, too, has "no purpose whatever," and his performance, like Hechingen's company, delights Hans Karl "much more than the wittiest talk of anybody on earth." Hans Karl's friendship for Hechingen is illuminated by the reply of a very different Austrian writer, Kafka, to the remark that a certain acquaintance was stupid. "To be stupid is human. Many clever people are not wise, and therefore in the last resort not even clever. They are merely inhuman out of fear of their own meaningless vulgarity." This meaningless vulgarity, of course, is represented in Hofmannsthal's play by the Famous Man, as well as by Neuhoff. The true antinomy everywhere in the play is not one between cleverness and stupidity, but between delicacy of feeling and a scheming vanity. The ultimate bond between Hechingen and Antoinette is that both have this delicacy of feeling, however differently it is manifested.

Hofmannsthal's counterpoint of ironies in this play includes both Neuhoff and the Famous Man, no less than Neugebauer. Their points of view are by no means to be discounted as purely negative or antagonistic. For all his partial self-identification with Hans Karl, Hofmannsthal's attitude to him necessarily involved a corresponding measure of self-irony. Neuhoff's strictures on Hans Karl and on the Viennese aristocracy always contain a substantial grain of truth, as well as reflecting Neuhoff's own resentment and frustration. As for the Famous Man, Hofmannsthal was far from wishing to justify either Edine's stupidity or the indifference of other characters to new developments in learning and art —contrasted here with Neuhoff's German reverence for "culture." Hofmannsthal was too conscious of another irony, that of his own situation in Austria. The notorious cultural conservatism of the Austrians prevented his own work from being recognized and understood; this very play was first performed in Germany. Hofmannsthal's place in Austrian society would have been not unlike the Famous Man's if Hofmannsthal had allowed personal vanity and snobbery to determine his attitudes.

As it was, he remained the Difficult Man and representative of a society that did not exist, using social, historical, and literary conventions as a frame for intimate enigma variations. Sigismund and Hans Karl define their range: the disinherited prince in his tower, carried from the dream of pre-existence into active life, struggling with it for the dream's sake, defeated; and the seemingly mundane man, seemingly at home and at ease in his social world, but secretly a perfectionist no less than Sigismund, ruled by a mystical absolute as a lover and a friend, opposing a necessity rooted in pre-existence to the improvisations, accidents, and machinations of active life. Ultimately, therefore, *The Difficult Man* is as difficult and mysterious a work as *The Tower;* and it is in its trivialities that Hofmannsthal attained the utmost refinement of his art.

NOTES

Except where other references are given, all quotations from Hofmannsthal's works are based on the fifteen-volume *Gesammelte Werke*, edited by Herbert Steiner, published by S. Fischer Verlag, Frankfurt a/M.

60. *Nietzsche:* "As you see, I am essentially antitheatrical by nature; for the theatre, that mass art *par excellence,* I have that scorn deep down in my soul that every artist has today. *Success* in the theatre—with that a man goes down in my esteem to the point of no recall; *failure*—there I prick up my ears and begin to respect." *Nietzsche contra Wagner* (1888).

Stefan George: See *Briefwechsel zwischen George und Hofmannsthal* (Munich, 1953), pp. 133–34.

George's attitude to music, and that of his followers, is the subject of G. R. Urban's study *Kinesis and Stasis* (The Hague, 1962). The Circle's antipathy to music, too, was anticipated by Nietzsche in his later writings, especially the polemics against Wagner, though Nietzsche's antipathy was neither wholehearted nor all-inclusive.

61. *Karl Wolfskehl:* Born at Darmstadt in 1869, first met Stefan George in 1893 and became one of his closest associates. He collaborated with George as joint editor of a series of selections from German writers admired by the Circle. In later life he emerged as a poet of original vision, and though always loyal to George's example and

memory, became closely identified with the Jewish tradition after 1933. He died at Auckland, New Zealand, in 1948.

See *The Correspondence between Richard Strauss and Hugo von Hofmannsthal,* with an introduction by Edward Sackville-West (London and New York, 1961; American edn.: *A Working Friendship*). The passages quoted are from pp. xx, 12, 49, 58, 77, 81, 108, and 109.

Harry Graf Kessler: See his *Tagebücher 1918–1937* (Frankfurt a/M, 1961), p. 589. Count Kessler, born in Paris in 1868, was active as a diplomat, patron of the arts, publisher, and lecturer in the cause of democracy. Together with his friend Aristide Maillol, the sculptor, he accompanied Hofmannsthal on his journey to Greece in 1908. Six years later he collaborated with Hofmannsthal in writing the dance scenario *Josephslegende* for Richard Strauss and Diaghilev. Kessler had to leave Germany after 1933 and died in a French village in 1937.

Bodenhausen: See *Hugo von Hofmannsthal, Eberhard von Bodenhausen: Briefe der Freundschaft* (Düsseldorf, 1953), p. 161. E. von Bodenhausen (1868–1918) was a lawyer, art critic, and industrialist. He was one of the founders of the literary periodical *Pan,* to which Hofmannsthal contributed, and became one of Hofmannsthal's closest friends.

65. *The Letter of Lord Chandos:* See the English version in *Selected Prose,* pp. 129–41. See also Donald Davie's comment on the Letter in his *Articulate Energy* (London, 1955), pp. 1–5.

66. *Essay on Paul Bourget:* See *Prosa I* (1956), p. 9.

Eleonora Duse: For Hofmannsthal's tribute to her, see *Prosa I,* p. 70.

The sense, not the words: Hofmannsthal, *Briefe 1890–1901* (Berlin, 1935), p. 42. The letter is to Felix Baron Oppenheimer.

67. *Between the fleeting fame:* From the *Book of Friends.* See *Selected Prose,* p. 352.

Poems on the deaths of actors: See *Poems and Verse Plays,* pp. 66–71 and 560. The translation of the poem on Mitterwurzer is by Stephen Spender.

69. *The stage as dream image:* For Hofmannsthal's note for his essay "Die Bühne als Traumbild" (1903), see my "Hofmannsthals Bibliothek," *Euphorion* (Heidelberg), LV (1961), 43.

70. *Space between characters:* See *Selected Prose,* p. 266.

Notes

Prologue to the "Antigone": See *Poems and Verse Plays,* pp. 545 and 541. The translator is Christopher Middleton.

72. *Kainz*: For the poem on this actor, see *Gedichte und lyrische Dramen* (1946), pp. 51–52.

73. *To have genius . . . :* See *Aufzeichnungen* (1959), p. 209. It has been suggested that the word "Unvernunft" (unreason) here is a misreading for "Urvernunft" (primal reason or *logos*), in which case the sense intended would be the opposite of the sense conveyed in the printed text. Because of a basic conflict in Hofmannsthal's own nature, either word seems plausible and in character.

74. *The shaped work . . . :* See Hofmannsthal's lecture (1922) on Grillparzer, *Prosa IV* (1955), p. 126.

"I"-suppression: See *Selected Prose,* p. xl.

75. *The Triumph of Time*: Though Strauss rejected this ballet libretto, it was eventually performed with music by Alexander von Zemlinsky (1872–1942), Austrian conductor and composer, and Schönberg's teacher, active in Vienna, Mannheim, Prague and Berlin. He emigrated in 1938 to New York.

Hofmannsthal also collaborated with the Austrian composer Egon Wellesz (born 1885), who composed the music for Hofmannsthal's ballet scenario *Achilles auf Skyros* in 1922 and for the opera *Alkestis,* based on Hofmannsthal's early adaptation of the play by Euripides. Part of the operatic version of this text (1923) was prepared by the composer.

Frank Kermode: See his essay "Poet and Dancer before Diaghilev" in his *Puzzles and Epiphanies* (London, 1962). The passage quoted is from p. 4, but the whole essay is relevant.

76. *Fear*: See *Selected Prose,* pp. 155–64. The translation is by Tania and James Stern.

77. *Oscar Wilde*: See Hofmannsthal's essay in *Prosa II* (1951), pp. 133–38. The passage quoted is on p. 138.

81. See *Hugo von Hofmannsthal–Carl J. Burckhardt: Briefwechsel* (Frankfurt a/M, 1957), p. 298.

83. *Postcard to Marie Herzfeld*: Unpublished; in the British Museum, Egerton MS. 3150. The card is undated, but the blurred postmark appears to read March 3, 1893.

84. *Song is marvellous . . . :* See *Aufzeichnungen,* p. 28.

86. *Mabel Collins*: Hofmannsthal's library contains a copy of

the third edition (London, 1910) of her *The Idyll of the White Lotus*, but he had previously read the work in an earlier edition. The allegory involves two "mysterious Queen" figures, one of whom is called the "spirit of light" or "Queen mother"; it is the other, associated with darkness and evil, whom Hofmannsthal mainly had in mind both in *The Mine at Falun* and in the sketches for *Jupiter and Semele*. Not only is Hofmannsthal's Queen of the Mountain more closely akin to Mabel Collins's dark Queen, but it is her evil High Priest Agmahd whose name Hofmannsthal borrowed for the attendant spirit in *The Mine at Falun*. (The source is dealt with in "Hofmannsthals Bibliothek," p. 59.)

E. M. Butler: See her article "Hofmannsthal's 'Elektra': A Graeco-Freudian Myth," *Journal of the Warburg Institute* (London), II:2 (1938). The passage quoted from Hermann Bahr is from his *Dialog vom Tragischen* (Berlin, 1904); in fact the book appeared in 1903, as *Electra* did also.

87. Hofmannsthal's comments on *Electra*: See *Aufzeichnungen*, pp. 217, 201, 131, and 237.

Ad me Ipsum: See *Aufzeichnungen*, pp. 211–44.

William H. Rey: See his *Weltentzweiung und Weltversöhnung in Hofmannsthals Griechischen Dramen* (Philadelphia, 1962), p. 36.

94. *In action, in deeds* . . . : From Hofmannsthal's notes for a lecture *The Idea of Europe* (1916) in *Prosa III* (1952), p. 378. Other remarks on *Electra* occur in the same volume, pp. 138, 139, 335, 353–55, and 365.

95. *Else Lasker-Schüler:* See her *Briefe an Karl Kraus* (Cologne and Berlin, n. d.), p. 82; and *Dichtungen und Dokumente* (Munich, n. d.), pp. 517–18.

96. Hofmannsthal on his *Everyman:* "Das Spiel vor der Menge," *Prosa III*, pp. 60–65; "Das Alte Spiel von Jedermann," ibid., pp. 114–32.

97. *The powerful imagination is conservative* . . . : See *Aufzeichnungen*, p. 41.

98. For details of Hofmannsthal's reading and annotation of these books, see "Hofmannsthals Bibliothek," pp. 31–35.

100. *Neo-Platonism:* Cf. introduction to *Poems and Verse Plays*, pp. xxxix–xl.

101. *The poet's starting point:* From a letter by Hofmannsthal to Fritz Setz, in *Corona* (Munich), X (1940), 6.

102. It was by Grimmelshausen's *Simplicissimus*, too, that Hofmannsthal's attention was drawn to the Spanish moralist Antonio de Guevara (1480–1545). Grimmelshausen's novel concludes with a long passage from Guevara that comprises the passages quoted in *The Tower*; but Hofmannsthal adapted Grimmelshausen's German translation.

107. *Bertolt Brecht:* A specific and curious parallel between the two dramatists can be found in Brecht's *Im Dickicht der Städte* (*In the Jungle of Cities*), written at about the same time as the early version of *The Tower* and first performed in Munich on May 9, 1923, and again in Berlin in 1924. A passage in Brecht's play (Scene 6)—"Now the crayfishes mate, the love-cry of the stags is in the thicket, and the badger can be hunted"—is extraordinarily like the opening of Basilius's speech about his past prowess in Act II of *The Tower*. Since Hofmannsthal does not appear to have seen Brecht's play performed, and since the play was not published until 1927—four years after the first publication of Hofmannsthal's passage—the borrowing, if any, must have been Brecht's.

The social side of his nature: In his retrospective postscript of 1927 to *Der Rosenkavalier*, in *Prosa IV*, pp. 426–30, Hofmannsthal remarks on the "social genesis" of this work in conversations with his friend Count Harry Kessler. These conversations seem to have taken the place of literary sources, and it is likely that Kessler helped Hofmannsthal to invent a plot. Hofmannsthal wrote another short comment on the libretto in 1911: "Ungeschriebenes Nachwort zum Rosenkavalier," *Prosa III*, pp. 43–45.

108. The original version of the second act of *Der Rosenkavalier* was published in *Die Neue Rundschau* (Frankfurt a/M), LXIV: 3 (1953), with a commentary by Willi Schuh.

110. *Maria Theresia:* See Hofmannsthal's essay in *Prosa III*, pp. 387–400. Hofmannsthal's notes on Maria Theresia in his copy of La Bruyère are transcribed in "Hofmannsthals Bibliothek," p. 46.

111. *Adam Müller:* (1779–1829) German Romantic political economist.

113. *Franz Tumler:* See his "Rosenkavalier und Arabella," *Neue Deutsche Hefte* (Gütersloh), No. 29 (September 1956).

116. *Anton Wildgans:* See *Der Briefwechsel Hofmannsthal–Wildgans* (Zurich, Munich, Paris, 1935), p. 52.

118. *Prussian and Austrian:* In *Prosa III*, pp. 407–9.

HOFMANNSTHAL'S DEBT TO THE ENGLISH-SPEAKING WORLD

HOFMANNSTHAL'S DEBT
TO THE ENGLISH-SPEAKING WORLD

THIS SUBJECT demands a few words of explanation, because it may seem far-fetched, tenuous, and marginal; but I think that a student of Hofmannsthal does well to ponder the words which Goethe addressed to the Physicist. Like Nature in Goethe's poem, Hofmannsthal had "neither core nor outer rind, being all things at once." And the corollary, too, applies to the Hofmannsthal scholar:

> It's yourself you should scrutinize to see
> Whether you're centre or periphery.

With Hofmannsthal, as with Goethe's Nature, "at every place we're at the centre," if only we beware of the temptation to lose sight of the centre in pursuing the astonishing wealth and variety of minute particulars on the periphery. Both in his work and his life Hofmannsthal believed in "concealing the depth in the surface"; once this peculiarity has been recognized, there is no part of the extensive surface of his mind that does not yield some intimation of the depth.

Writing on Hofmannsthal and England more than thirty years ago, Dr. Mary Gilbert found it "perplexing" that this writer, whose "Europe was the Catholic Europe of the baroque period"[1] should himself have laid such great emphasis on his debt to "northern and Protestant England." If we turn to a more

[1] Mary E. Gilbert, "Hofmannsthal and England," *German Life and Letters,* I (1937), 182-193.

recent view of Hofmannsthal, in Professor Fritz Martini's history of German Literature, we also read that Hofmannsthal "lived deeply within the Catholic-Baroque heritage of Vienna"; but Professor Martini goes on to say that "the Middle Ages and the Baroque, Venice and Florence, Spain, classical antiquity and the Orient" were Hofmannsthal's "spiritual home." If to this "spiritual home," or to these spiritual homes, we add Germany, France, the Low Countries, Britain, America, Scandinavia and Eastern Europe, all of which made significant contributions to Hofmannsthal's work and development, we are coming closer to the complex truth of the matter.

Although she appeared to accept the more exclusive view of Hofmannsthal, Dr. Gilbert very clearly demonstrated that Hofmannsthal's affinity with "the Catholic Europe of the baroque period" was far from being his only one. In quoting the following passage from Hofmannsthal's letter to Felix Baron Oppenheimer of 4th April 1899, she was the first to draw attention to a very different source:

In my imaginative life London occupies a vast space: more threads than I can enumerate run out from there, and the most important influences on my inner life can be traced more or less directly to English art, English ways of thinking or the intense and world-encompassing contemporary life that is concentrated there. [2]

Before going on to particularize and substantiate this indication of Hofmannsthal's—and there is more evidence for it than can be adduced here—I must return very briefly to the larger question of perspective. It is certainly true that in later life, after 1916 to be precise, Hofmannsthal tended to stress his links with "the Catholic Europe of the baroque period" and, guided in part by the theories of Professor Josef Nadler, to see himself primarily as a late representative of the Bavarian-Austrian or

[2] *Briefe 1890-1901* (Leipzig, 1935), p. 285.

134

South German theatrical tradition. [3] Yet to pin Hofmannsthal down to this single tradition—if indeed it is a single tradition— would be as wrong as to assume a radical change of heart or outlook on his part between the early statement just quoted and the later ones. For all his complexity and diversity, few writers were more consistent than Hofmannsthal. Only by balancing one statement against another, with constant reference to the whole of his work and its centre, can we avoid violating either the complexity or the consistency; and it is the two together that constitute Hofmannsthal's chief distinction among the imaginative writers of his time.

Hofmannsthal's consistency in this matter of his relation- ship to England can be shown by citing three other passages written at various times in his life; the first as early as June 1894, at the age of twenty, the last in February 1929, only a few months before his death at the age of fifty-five. The first two are from his notebooks:

English aestheticism as the element of our culture. I. First en- counter: as a curiosity, perhaps some affectation, fancy dress etc. II. Oscar Wilde, "Intentions": a strong narcotic charm, sophistically seductive, inelegantly paradoxical, reaction against English utili- tarianism. III. Ruskin, Pater, Madox Brown, Rossetti, Burne-Jones —those deep connections with the life of the soul, the whole an attempt to an inward culture. [4]

Here, in a nutshell, we have Hofmannsthal's own account of his early debt to English art and literature, that is, to the Eng- lish aesthetic movement and its various representatives; that this account is not uncritical of the influence points to an inner

[3] See *Prosa* IV (1955), 324-325, and passim. [References to Hof- mannsthal's works in this essay are to the fifteen-volume *Gesammelte Werke*, edited by Herbert Steiner, published by S. Fischer Verlag, Frankfurt a/M.]

[4] *Aufzeichnungen* (1959), 108.

conflict also present in Hofmannsthal's playlets of the same period, as well as in his critical essays on Pater, [5] Wilde, Swinburne and many other contemporary writers. It is worth noting, too, that Hofmannsthal ascribes the excesses of the aesthetic movement to a reaction against utilitarianism; even at the age of twenty he had a sharp eye for political and cultural realities. Hofmannsthal's notebook for the same year contains quotations from poems by Browning—another important influence on his work—and there is another entry on Browning in the following year. In July of that year, 1895, he returned to the subject of aestheticism in a longer entry, from which I shall quote only a few relevant extracts:

Great beginnings, depravation now. —A circular traffic, growing by reciprocity, at once enticing and pernicious, between England, Belgium, France. Arts draw closer together, farther away from the public . . . —The first effect from England (Rossetti) . . . Swinburne a culmination; now the sophistication of young half-talents. —Pater already a morbid hypertrophy of critcism. . . . [6]

The still more censorious tone of this passage does not mean that Hofmannsthal had broken once and for all with English aestheticism, or aestheticism in general; the words "at once enriching and pernicious" render the conflict in his own mind between its attractive and repellent qualities. How crucial this conflict remained for at least another decade, how many of Hofmannsthal's works sprang from the tension between a sensuous and an ethical impulse, cannot be elaborated here; but his debt to English aestheticism is inseparable from this central preoccupation.

[5] It is significant, too, that for his essay on Pater of 1894 Hofmannsthal chose the pseudonym "Archibald O'Hagan, B.A.—Old Rookery, Herfordshire" [sic].

[6] *Aufzeichnungen*, 123.

The last passage is from Hofmannsthal's letter of 20th February 1929 to his friend Professor Walther Brecht, most of which is devoted to an account of his relationship with Stefan George. Hofmannsthal wrote here of his early encounter with George:

Summing up, one can say that the encounter was of decisive importance—the confirmation of my own potentialities, proof that I was not an egregious crank to believe in the possibility of doing something in the German language that would move on the same level as the great Englishman after Keats, yet would be related, on the other hand, to the strict forms of the Romance literatures. [1]

Even at the end of his life, then, Hofmannsthal regarded his early poetry as an attempt to emulate the "great Englishmen after Keats"; and he did not regard this influence as opposed to that of Romance literature and culture on his development, because these in turn had so greatly influenced the English poets of the nineteenth century.

The eminence of these poets alone explains why Hofmannsthal attached such great importance to them. However, since Hofmannsthal chose to study Romance languages and literatures at Vienna University, and came close to an academic appointment in this discipline, his emphasis on English literature may still seem astonishing. The most important circumstance to be borne in mind is that Hofmannsthal's scholarly and antiquarian interests were always subordinated to his needs as a poet and writer; another is that whatever his spiritual homes may have been, Hofmannsthal's immediate starting-point was the world in which he grew up and the literary culture of his own time. This culture was cosmopolitan and liberal; and the British component in it was very pervasive. Moreover, Hof-

---

[1] *Der Briefwechsel zwischen George und Hofmannsthal* (Düsseldorf, 1953), pp. 235-236.

mannsthal's attitude to the aestheticism of the eighteen-nineties was characterized by those reservations which were to determine his later development. English aestheticism differed from the French in one important respect; from Gautier onwards, the French advocates of "Art for Art's sake" had deliberately and progressively widened the gulf between "art" and "life," art and society—the very gulf of which Hofmannsthal complains in his notebook entry of 1895. Hofmannsthal's difference with Stefan George hinged on the same issue. In his essays of the same period on English art and literature Hofmannsthal repeatedly commented on the ethical and social aspects of English aestheticism—"die englische ästhetisch-moralische Form," as he called it—in contrast with the greater sensuousness of the French school. Thus, in the essay *Über Englische Malerei* of 1894, in connection with Ruskin and the Pre-Raphaelites, Hofmannsthal observed: "Besides, this English art of psychic-physical beauty is thoroughly ethical."[8] Where the English aesthetes, too, tended towards the doctrine of an autonomous aestheticism, like Walter Pater in the Third Book of *Marius the Epicurean,* or cultivated a hypertrophy of the senses, like Swinburne in much of his poetry, Hofmannsthal did not exempt them from his general critique of modern decadence.

Dr. Gilbert has already given a fully documented account of what the English way of life meant to Hofmannsthal ever since his adolescence:

He behaved like an Englishman, in francophile Vienna. . . . He laid stress on the fact that he was acquainted with members of the British Embassy in Vienna; he played tennis rather ostentatiously, when the game had not yet become fashionable on the Continent. He was so well acquainted with English customs as to promise his friend Bahr English recipes. He alluded to the habit of sending Christmas cards; he imitated English headings of letters and inter-

[8] *Prosa* I (1950), 233.

spersed his own letters with English words. . . . He was attracted to the idea of the "gentleman," in which he saw his own ideal of a cultured life personified. [9]

Dr. Gilbert cited the *Letter of Lord Chandos* and the *Briefe des Zurückgekehrten* as examples of how this conception of the gentleman entered into Hofmannsthal's imaginative works; and she quoted the following definition of the gentleman from Hofmannsthal's letter to Edgar Freiherr Karg von Bebenburg of 21st August 1894: "I think the deepest sense of what is meant by the word gentleman is that one should be better and more noble than life." [10] On the other hand, it is only fair to add, Hofmannsthal's very early essay *Englisches Leben,* published when he was seventeen, contains this comment on the biography of the English adventurer and occultist Laurence Oliphant; "And all of England's spirit is in this book, with its riches and its limitations, lacking the topmost heights and the lowest depths." [11]

English life continued to fascinate Hofmannsthal during the next decade of his life. His library contains a copy of the second edition of *An Onlooker's Notebook* (London, 1902), a collection of sociological articles from the *Manchester Guardian,* which he read and annotated in December 1904. He was especially interested in the sections dealing with economics; thus he referred in a note to a passage on 'Manchesterism,' which the writer defined as "unrestricted competition, every man for himself, 'the devil take the hindmost' and the survival of the fittest." A second note of Hofmannsthal's in this book refers to the historical origins of this trend in the eighteenth century: "Pitt declares that everybody with £1000 a year has the right to a peerage." Another English book that Hofmanns-

---

[9] Gilbert, *op. cit.*

[10] *Briefe 1890-1901*, p. 113.   [11] *Prosa* I, 72.

thal read with care at this time, in June 1906, was *A Modern Symposium* by G. Lowes Dickinson. The many passages marked by Hofmannsthal in his copy of this work show that he was no less interested in the Socialist point of view than in the Conservative. Hofmannsthal also marked a passage about a possible synthesis of the two points of view and the creation of a "Tory-Socialist party." A passage on the artist's plight in democracies is especially heavily marked; but against an attack on the philistinism of America Hofmannsthal has entered the words "Poe! Whitman!" in protest. At the back of the book he has noted "culture!"—meaning the high cultural level of Lowes Dickinson's book, and of England generally—but also: "Inequality—the whole country full of it." Hofmannsthal's interest in economic questions and the evils of capitalism is confirmed by several other books in his library.

Little has become known as yet about Hofmannsthal's visits to England or his relations with British friends and acquaintances such as Robert Vansittart, Edward Gordon Craig, Cyril Scott, Ethel Smyth, John Drinkwater, and Gilbert Murray. (Hofmannsthal visited Brighton and London in 1900, London again in 1925. Both visits were brief.) Scattered references in his works and published letters suggest that personal contacts with English and American men and women were as important to him as his wide acquaintance with English literature and English institutions. There is the Englishwoman of *Erinnerung Schöner Tage* (1907), "one of those Englishwomen who are like classical statues. Marvellous, that youthful radiance of her almost severe features and the curve of her eyebrows that were shaped like wings." [12] Hofmannsthal's notebook of 1908 records one of his meetings with the young Bos-

---

[12] *Prosa* II (1951), 403-406.

tonian Gladys D.,[13] of whom he writes that she was "in certain ways the most striking person that I have ever met. . . . Among twenty-five people she alone always dominates the conversation; flatters, insults, penetrates. The quickness and elasticity of her mind are astounding."[14] In a plan for his periodical *Neue Deutsche Beiträge,* drafted about 1920, Hofmannsthal names Gilbert Murray, Lowes Dickinson, and Granville Barker among the prospective contributors and describes them as "die bedeutenden reingesinnten Engländer."[15]

To such references we can add the evidence of the Rodaun Visitors' Book, which records visits by Cyril Scott, Ethel Smyth, and Robert Vansittart, as well as the American dancer Ruth St. Denis. Hofmannsthal's association with Edward Gordon Craig was mainly professional, and 'theatre business' thwarted most of their projects for collaboration. In 1906 Craig presented Hofmannsthal with a copy of his book *The Art of the Theatre* with the inscription "To the Poet in all admiration." This admiration is borne out by Craig's unpublished letters to Hofmannsthal—whom he called "the most intelligent man in Germany"—and it also transpires from these that Craig wanted Hofmannsthal to write a preface to the German edition of his book.

The letters of Arthur Symons to Hofmannsthal reveal that it was Mrs. Patrick Campbell who asked him to translate Hofmannsthal's *Elektra;* unfortunately their correspondence was confined to practical matters arising over the translation, and

[13] Gladys Deacon, who became the ninth Duchess of Marlborough. Cf. Hofmannsthal's letter to Helene von Nostitz of 31 July 1908. Hugo von Hofmannsthal and Helene von Nostitz, *Briefwechsel* (Frankfurt, 1965), pp. 70-71.

[14] *Aufzeichnungen,* 160-161.

[15] *Ibid.,* 367.

there is no reason to suppose that Hofmannsthal knew of Symons' importance as a link between the French Symbolists, the English poets of the 'nineties and such twentieth century writers as W. B. Yeats, James Joyce, and Ezra Pound. Hofmannsthal's unpublished papers also include letters from Granville Barker, Ethel Smyth, Cyril Scott, John Galsworthy, Gilbert Murray, and other English acquaintances; his library, inscribed copies of books by Robert Vansittart and John Drinkwater. Hofmannsthal had some correspondence with T. S. Eliot over a contribution to *The Criterion;* and Eliot's *The Sacred Wood* is still extant among the books in Hofmannsthal's library. Incomplete though they are, these names may suffice to indicate the range of Hofmannsthal's personal associations with England; it is characteristic of him that they should have included representatives not only of all the arts, but of diplomacy and the world of learning.

The extent of Hofmannsthal's reading in English was such that only a rough general outline can be given here, followed by a few instances of borrowings, influences, and parallels. As one would expect from indications in his notebooks and letters, the nineteenth century writers are prominent in his library. Besides the poetry of Coleridge, Wordsworth, Byron, Keats and Shelley, Poe, Whitman, Browning, and Swinburne, he read Coleridge's letters, Lamb's and De Quincey's essays, the *Imaginary Conversations* of Walter Savage Landor, novels by Jane Austen, Dickens and Conrad, various prose works by Ruskin, Pater, Wilde, and Yeats. The poets after Milton and before Blake do not appear to have interested him; but the eighteenth century is represented by Sheridan's comedies, Addison's essays, Gibbon's *Decline and Fall,* the letters of Horace Walpole and Lord Chesterfield, Boswell's *Life of Johnson,* novels by Defoe, Smollett, Sterne, and Fielding, and William Beckford's *Vathek.*

Hofmannsthal's knowledge of Shakespeare and Francis Bacon needs no emphasis; his interest in the sixteenth and seventeenth centuries led him to study many minor Elizabethan, Jacobean and Restoration dramatists, including Dekker, Beaumont and Fletcher, Ford, Webster, Thomas Middleton, Philip Massinger, Thomas Shadwell, Vanbrugh, Otway, and Congreve. Of seventeenth-century prose works, Burton's *Anatomy of Melancholy* is extant in Hofmannsthal's library.

Adaptations of Coleridge's *Fact and Phantom* and of Browning's *A Serenade at the Villa* are to be found among Hofmannsthal's poems,[16] the former among the few which Hofmannsthal published in his lifetime. As late as 1901 Hofmannsthal also worked on a play, *Pompilia oder das Leben,* on a subject derived from Browning's *The Ring and the Book.* What is much more significant, it was mainly to Browning's example that Hofmannsthal owed the very idea of both lyrical drama and those dramatic monologues and studies which he called *Gestalten.* If we consider that these two intermediate genres enabled Hofmannsthal to make the difficult transition from an essentially lyrical to an essentially dramatic output, it is to Browning, above all, that we should apply Hofmannsthal acknowledgement to the English poets after Keats. Hofmannsthal read Browning's work repeatedly after 1892; his copy of *Poems by Robert Browning* (London, 1898) records the dates of 1903, 1905, 1913, and 1925.

In other respects, it is true, Hofmannsthal's affinity with Keats himself is more apparent than his affinity with Browning. The following lines from Keats's poem "On Death," for instance, are strikingly close in mood and tone to the concluding lines of *Der Tor und der Tod:*

> How strange it is that man on earth should roam,

[16] *Gedichte* (1946), 93 and 23, respectively.

And lead a life of woe, but not forsake
His rugged path . . .

Wie wundervoll sind diese Wesen,
Die, was nicht deutbar, dennoch deuten,
Was nie geschrieben wurde, lesen,
Verworrenes beherrschend binden
Und Wege noch im Ewig-Dunklen finden.

(Strange are these creatures, strange indeed,
Who what's unfathomable, fathom,
What never yet was written, read,
Knit and command the tangled mystery
And in the eternal dark yet find a way.)

as well as to the following lines from "Ballade des Ausseren Lebens":

Was frommt das alles uns und diese Spiele
Die wir doch gross und ewig einsam sind
Und wandernd nimmer suchen irgend Ziele?

(What does it profit us, and all these games,
Who, great and lonely, ever shall be so
And though we always wander seek no aims?)

The edition of *The Poetical Works of John Keats* in Hofmannsthal's library was published in 1892. Hofmannsthal's notes in the book suggest that he read the shorter poems at about this time, though he read 'The Eve of St. Agnes,' 'Isabella' and 'Lamia' as late as 1912, when he also marked the poem 'Welcome joy and welcome sorrow' with a note for *Die Frau ohne Schatten:* "for the Emperor/what he withheld from the Empress."

Hofmannsthal's most extraordinary and substantial debt to Keats has only recently come to light, and it is of so unusual a kind that it gave its discoverer, Professor Herman Meyer, occasion for fascinating reflections on what he calls "the spirit of verse."[17] What Professor Meyer revealed is that Hofmannsthal's most tantalizingly elusive poem, his *Lebenslied* of 1896—to the interpretation of which Professor Richard Exner devoted a whole book in 1964[18]—is a formal, though not a thematic, imitation of Keat's *Stanzas* beginning:

> In a drear-nighted December,
>   Too happy, happy tree,
> Thy branches ne'er remember
>   Their green felicity:
> The north cannot undo them
> With a sleety whistle through them;
> Nor frozen thawings glue them
>   From budding at the prime.

That Hofmannsthal could take over the peculiar rhythmic structure of this poem for a composition that has little else in common with it and wholly avoids the slightly comic effect inherent in the triple feminine rhymes of the fifth, sixth, and seventh lines tells us a great deal about his distinction as a lyrical poet and about the *Lebenslied* in particular; but here it is more relevant to stress the intense receptivity with which he must have read the poems of Keats at an early age.

Another English influence on the poems goes back to Hofmannsthal's childhood, when he owned picture books by Kate Greenaway, as we learn from the early autobiographical piece to which he gave the English title *Age of Innocence*.[19] In the

---

[17] Herman Meyer, "On the Spirit of Verse." In: *The Disciplines of Criticism, Essays in Literary Theory, Interpretation, and History, Honoring René Wellek on His Sixty-Fifth Birthday* (New Haven, 1968), pp. 331-347.

[18] *Hugo von Hofmannsthal's "Lebenslied," eine Studie* (Heidelberg, 1964).

[19] *Prosa* I, 147.

slightly later essay *Englischer Stil* of 1896 [20] he writes in connection with a performance by the Barrison sisters:

When the Barrisons enter one expects that on the dusty music-
hall stage, behind their yellow hair and childish shoulders, the
moon will rise too, that oversized Japanese full moon, as in Kate
Greenaway's children's books behind the five schoolgirls with yellow hair, baby bonnets and pink gowns.

It is not difficult to recognize the same association once more
in the second and third parts of Hofmannsthal's 'Terzinen über
Vergänglichkeit,' written some two years before the essay, but
quite especially in these lines:

> Und Träume schlagen so die Augen auf
> Wie kleine Kinder unter Kirschenbäumen,
>
> Aus deren Krone den blassgoldnen Lauf
> Der Vollmond anhebt durch die grosse Nacht.
>
> (Our dreams as suddenly open wide their eyes
> As little children under cherry-trees
>
> Out of whose crests the full moon mounts the skies
> On her pale golden course through the great night.)

The same childhood association may account for Hofmannsthal's emphasis on the virginal, youthful or androgynous character of English art and style generally, what he calls their
"merkwürdige Kindlichkeit" in the essay—a quality which he
also sensed in the work of the Pre-Raphaelite painters. In the
same essay Hofmannsthal speaks of the design of tennis clothes,
furniture and picture books as examples of English style. Since
it was one of the foremost aims of the aesthetic movement to
effect a synthesis of all the arts, it is not surprising that a visual
association should have had such power over him. A thorough
examination of Hofmannsthal's imagery in this light would
almost certainly reveal other debts to English graphic and

[20] *Ibid.,* 292.

decorative art. Walter Crane and Aubrey Beardsley were among the English illustrators whom he admired. The sketches for his unfinished tragedy on the *Pentheus* theme (1904) begin with an epigraph from Walter Pater and the note: "Costumes in the spirit of Aubrey Beardsley."[21]

Richard Alewyn[22] has remarked on the implications for Hofmannsthal not so much of the work as of the fate of Oscar Wilde, whom in the essay *Sebastian Melmoth* of 1905 Hofmannsthal celebrated as a tragic hero of the age: "Oscar Wilde's character and Oscar Wilde's fate are one and the same thing. He went towards his downfall with such strides as Oedipus the seeing and blind. The aesthete was tragic. The fop was tragic. . . . He defied reality. And he felt how life crouched to leap upon him out of the dark."[23] No contemporary writer was more aware of both the temptations and the perils of extreme aestheticism than Hofmannsthal; his early playlets and stories are variations on this theme. It was Oscar Wilde who asserted that life imitates art; and, as Professor Alewyn has shown, Oscar Wilde's fate is prefigured in Hofmannsthal's magnificent story of the merchant's son, *The Tale of the 672nd Night*, published in 1895, before Oscar Wilde's trial and fall. This strange concordance, then, is not one of literary influence; rather it is to be ascribed to the *Zeitgeist* itself, and to the intuitive and imaginative power that enabled Hofmannsthal to grasp and interpret it.

The same is almost certainly true of the remarkable parallels between certain works of Hofmannsthal and certain works by his Irish contemporary W. B. Yeats. Since I have already dealt

[21] *Dramen* II (1954), 523.

[22] Richard Alewyn, *Über Hugo von Hofmannsthal* (Göttingen, 1958), pp. 143-144.

[23] *Prosa* II, 135

with some of the more striking of these parallels, I shall only confirm here that Hofmannsthal does not appear to have known these works by Yeats at the time. Much later, in 1916, Yeats's German translator Friedrich Eckstein presented Hofmannsthal with an inscribed copy of his selection of prose works by Yeats, *Erzählungen und Essays* (Leipzig, 1916), now the property of Dr. J. C. Middleton. Hofmannsthal read this book with care and marked many passages that shed light on his affinity with Yeats, as well as on their common debt to the English Romantics, Neo-Platonist thought, theosophy and Symbolist aesthetics. It is from this book also that Hofmannsthal took the two quotations from William Blake which he included in his *Buch der Freunde*.[24] Hofmannsthal's only published reference to Yeats occurs in his 'Vienna Letter' of 1922, written for the American periodical *The Dial*; there he spoke with sympathy of Yeats's endeavours to found an Irish National Theatre that would provide both for an educated and an uneducated public, compared this undertaking with the more favourable conditions in Vienna, with its long tradition of popular drama, and quotes from one of Yeats's early reports on his and Lady Gregory's work for the Irish Literary Theatre.[25] It is possible that Edward Gordon Craig, who was associated with both poets, gave Hofmannsthal an idea of Yeats's theatrical aspirations, although neither poet refers to the other in his published correspondence, and no book of poems or plays by Yeats is extant in Hofmannsthal's library. Both poets adapted parts of Sophocles's Oedipus trilogy for the modern stage. Hofmannsthal's dramatic fragment *Leda und der Schwan* constitutes one of an

[24] *Aufzeichnungen,* 45 and 48 and *Dramen* III (1957), 458.

[25] Hofmannsthal's quotation is from Yeats's essay "The Theatre" of 1899, reprinted in W. B. Yeats, *Essays and Introductions* (London, 1961). The passage in question is to be found on p. 167.

extraordinary number of thematic parallels with poems and plays by Yeats. The influence of Walter Pater on both poets— and quite especially of his passage on the Mona Lisa which Yeats thought important enough to place at the head of his *Oxford Book of Modern Verse*—was another link between them.

Because of his habit of appropriating and adapting not only whole works, but isolated lines, thoughts, metaphors and images taken from the works of his predecessors, Hofmannsthal's poems and plays abound in evidence of his wide reading. Those who assert that Hofmannsthal's originality and creative energy declined after his youth are also apt to assume that this practice is more marked in his later work than in the earlier; but the poems and playlets which he wrote in the 'nineties are as rich in direct and indirect borrowings as the comedies and libretti of his maturity. This applies to his reading in English also; as early as June 1892, even before the first mention of Browning in his letters, Hofmannsthal writes of using "a technical requisite from Shakespeare" for his unfinished Renaissance tragedy *Ascanio und Gioconda*.[26] The ten-volume edition of Shakespeare in Hofmannsthal's library (ed. Singer, 3rd Edition, London, 1883) corroborates his concern with Shakespeare's stagecraft. To cite only one instance: in Act III, Scene III of *Othello*, against Iago's "My lord, I take my leave," followed by the direction "Going" and Othello's next words: "Why did I marry?", Hofmannsthal has entered the words: "fausse sortie." At the back of the same volume Hofmannsthal has entered sketches for his comedy *Cristinas Heimreise*. In 1892 also, at the age of eighteen, Hofmannsthal had begun to study the dramatic works of Ford, Webster, and Massinger.

Hofmannsthal's borrowings or plagiarisms, as some would

---

[26] *Briefe 1890-1901,* p. 44.

call them, are a controversial matter; all that need be said here is that his practice rested on the deep and constant conviction that there can and should be no such thing as private property in literature. In many cases his unacknowledged quotations or translations must be construed as tributes to the authors and works he admires; in others, as something that belonged to Hofmannsthal as much, and in the same way, as the air he breathed or the streets in which he walked. To give an example of the former kind, in his lecture *Shakespeare's Könige und Grosse Herren* of 1905, Hofmannsthal praises the lines in which Brutus apologizes to Lucius for shortening his sleep: "How he apologizes for shortening his sleep, to which his youth has so great a claim."[27]. Hofmannsthal must be referring to these lines from Act IV, Scene III of *Julius Caesar:*

> I should not urge thy duty past thy might;
> I know young bloods look for a time of rest.

In Hofmannsthal's own tragedy *Oedipus und die Sphinx,* published in the following year, Creon says to the Boy[28]:

> Sleep on, young blood
> has need of sleep.

Clearly, Hofmannsthal felt no guilt over such stolen goods, since he himself drew attention to the appropriation in this case. In the same lecture Hofmannsthal remarked about Claudio in *Measure for Measure:* "How death squeezes the best juice out of him."[29] The remark applies equally well to Hofmannsthal's Claudio in *Der Tor und der Tod;* and it was no accident that Hofmannsthal chose this name for the man enclosed, immured and isolated within his own egotism. It seems likely, too, that the name Faninal in *Der Rosenkavalier* is an anagram of the

[27] *Prosa* II, 168.
[28] *Dramen* II, 329.
[29] *Prosa* II, 156.

name Fainall in Congreve's *The Way of the World,* though
here the connection is more tenuous.

Another Shakespeare echo, also connected with sleep, occurs
in *Der Abenteurer und die Sängerin,*[30] when Lorenzo says:

> Nun schon ich ihren Schlaf—und bald vielleicht
> Ermord ich ihr den Schlaf von vielen Nächten—
>
> (Now I respect her sleep—and soon perhaps
> Shall murder it, her sleep of many nights)

an obvious reminiscence of "Macbeth has murdered sleep." It
would seem, in fact, that English poetry is quite especially
prodigal of allusions to sleep, or that Hofmannsthal found it so.
In his playlet *Der Weisse Fächer*[31] the Mulatto Woman says:

> Denn was hat Schlaf mit Nacht zu tun, was Jugend
> Mit Treue?
>
> (For what has sleep to do with night, or youth
> With faithfulness?)

linking a new train of thought to a literal translation of Milton's
line from *Comus:*

> What hath night to do with sleep?

Hofmannsthal's knowledge of Milton's poetry is attested by an
entry in his notebook in 1911 and by a short note which he
entered in his copy of Boswell's *Johnson,* one of Hofmannsthal's favourite English books. Since there is no evidence that
Hofmannsthal knew William Blake's poetry at this early period,
one cannot be quite sure about the following lines from *Das
Bergwerk zu Falun*[32]:

> Du kannst das Glück nicht in verschlossnen Höhlen
> Dir halten, denn es atmet nur im Flug!

[30] *Dramen* I (1953), 225.
[31] *Gedichte,* 250.
[32] *Gedichte,* 377.

(You cannot bind joy fast to you in sealed
Cavern or dungeon; only in flight it breathes.)

but these lines certainly suggest that Hofmannsthal had read
Blake's *Eternity*, perhaps in an anthology.

He who binds to himself a joy
Does the winged life destroy;
But he who kisses the joy as it flies
Lives in eternity's sun rise.

If we add Hofmannsthal's adaptations of *Everyman* and *Venice
Preserv'd,* or his film scenario based on the life and works of
Daniel Defoe, to a great variety of concealed allusions and borrowings, the English background of his most revealing confession, the *Chandos Letter,* and of his projected imaginary
conversation *Essex und sein Richter,* to the many references
to English works in his essays, Hofmannsthal's debt to England
becomes very substantial indeed. The influence of Landor on
the dialogue form of some of Hofmannsthal's finest essays, and
of English criticism generally on all of them, are other matters
that would repay study. Hofmannsthal himself acknowledged
the superiority of English journalism,[33] using this word in a
sense neither derogatory nor patronizing, since he included
H. G. Wells, the "philosophical journalist," Lowes Dickinson
and the "poetic journalist" Lafcadio Hearn in this category,
just as he would have included his own essays.

Lafcadio Hearn is one of several authors to whom Hofmannsthal was indebted for his knowledge of the East; his library
contains other works by English orientalists, travellers and
translators from oriental languages, such as Arthur Waley's
translations of Chinese poems. The importance to him of Ka-
kasu Okakura's *The Ideals of the East, with special reference
to the Art of Japan* (London, 1903), a marked copy of which

[33] *Prosa* II, 299.

is extant in his library, becomes apparent in Hofmannsthal's notes for his lecture *Die Idee Europa* of 1916. [34]

The works of two British classical scholars, Gilbert Murray and J. W. Mackail, were no less important to him, as his notes in copies of their books testify. Hofmannsthal read Gilbert Murray's *The Rise of the Greek Epic* in 1912; besides marking many passages on Homer and Hesiod, he used the blank pages at the back for sketches later incorporated in the most outstanding of his own works bearing on classical antiquity, *Augenblicke in Griechenland*. Of the passages marked, two are especially interesting as indirect comments on Hofmannsthal's own peculiarities; and one of these peculiarities was to mark passages especially relevant to himself. "First of all," Murray writes, "I think we are apt to confuse originality with a much less important thing, novelty"—a distinction also made by Hofmannsthal. The relevance of the other passage to Hofmannsthal is equally clear: "And it is very noteworthy how many great poets seem to have drawn most of their inspiration not directly from experience, but derivatively from experience already interpreted by other men's poetry." Gilbert Murray's *A History of Ancient Greek Literature,* also in Hofmannsthal's library, was published in 1911; and so was the edition of Mackail's *Lectures on Greek Poetry* which Hofmannsthal read in 1912, and again in 1916. This work, too, occupied Hofmannsthal's attention at the time of his work on *Augenblicke in Griechenland*.

What Hofmannsthal wrote in 1899 about the many threads running out from London, and the important influences on his mental life, applies to every period of his life, from childhood to maturity. It may well be that the most vital of these influences have evaded me here, because they are not attached

---

[34] *Prosa* III (1952), 380.

to specific authors, works and references, but to moments of vision—epiphanies, as Joyce called them—to auras and associations. Thus, in the essay *Der Dichter und diese Zeit,* one is struck by an unexpected evocation of London itself, not unlike certain passages in T. S. Eliot's *The Waste Land* in its power to illuminate by sudden juxtaposition: "He is the most passionate admirer," Hofmannsthal writes of the poet, "of those things that are of eternity and those things that are of today. London in the fog with ghostly processions of the unemployed, the temple ruins of Luxor, the plashing of a remote woodland spring, the roaring of monstrous machines: transitions never give him any trouble."

Here London becomes the very paradigm of the modern city and the modern age, its unemployed like those spirits of whom T. S. Eliot, quoting Dante, was to write:

Unreal city,
Under the brown fog of a winter dawn,
A crowd flowed over London Bridge, so many,
I had not thought death had undone so many.

Whether or not Hofmannsthal's vision of London in the fog was a reminiscence of immediate experience—as "the ruined temples of Luxor" were not, since Hofmannsthal did not visit North Africa until 1925—may be of biographical interest, but it is quite irrelevant to an appreciation of his art. What matters in the case of either passage, Hofmannsthal's and Eliot's, is not the extent of the poet's reading and borrowings, but his capacity to absorb and organize disparate material, fuse immediate with vicarious experience, and make those transitions which give them new life and meaning.

It is in this light that Hofmannsthal's debt to English literature and English institutions should be considered. Exciting though it is to discover that the Captain in Hofmannsthal's comedy *Cristinas Heimreise* owes much of his past life to the real experiences of an English sailor in the year 1689, of which Hofmannsthal read in a twentieth century work by an American—William James's *The Varieties of Religious Experience*— what is much more important is that no one would have guessed as much without stumbling on the evidence. The transitions have been made with the utmost delicacy of thought and imagination, and the alien material naturalized to the wholly different atmosphere of Hofmannsthal's play.

Nevertheless, and granted that Hofmannsthal's debt to England and America was one of many debts to other nations and cultures, the extent of his interests and sympathies should never be left out of account in determining his status, allegiances and "spiritual home." These have been, and still are, persistently misrepresented by those who cannot or will not allow for his liberality and comprehensiveness of mind. Hofmannsthal was more than a "good European"; he attempted nothing less than to attain and uphold a Goethean universality in an age of which Yeats wrote:

> Things fall apart; the centre cannot hold;
> Mere anarchy is loosed upon the world.
> The blood-dimmed tide is loosed, and everywhere
> The ceremony of innocence is drowned;
> The best lack all conviction, while the worst
> Are full of passionate intensity.

To this state of anarchy Hofmannsthal struggled to oppose a "passionate intensity" quite unlike the fanaticism of "the worst," a passionate intensity tempered with understanding, committed to the centre and yet as all-embracing as the other is exclusive and destructive. Hofmannsthal's concern with the English-speaking world was part of that larger concern.

OTHER TITLES IN LITERATURE
AVAILABLE IN PRINCETON AND
PRINCETON/BOLLINGEN PAPERBACKS